Three-Minute Bible Stories Using Familiar Objects

by Marilyn Senterfitt

illustrated by Paul Konsterlie

Cover by Dan Grossman

Copyright © 1993

Shining Star Publications

ISBN No. 0-86653-760-0

Standardized Subject Code TA ac

Printing No. 9876543

Shining Star Publications
1204 Buchanan St., Box 299
Carthage, IL 62321-0299

Unless otherwise indicated, the New International Version of the Bible was used in preparing the activities in this book.

INTRODUCTION

Have you told any Bible stories lately? Did you tell about Noah building a great boat, David fighting Goliath, or Jesus feeding five thousand with five loaves and two fish? *How* did you tell the story? Perhaps you held up a large teaching picture, maybe you just read the story from the Bible, or told it in your own words. Bible stories have a drama all their own, but often they lose their freshness when children hear them again and again. This book offers an objective approach to sharing the familiar stories of the Old and New Testaments. Each begins with an everyday object that will be easy to obtain. It ends–hopefully and prayerfully–with smiling children!

Each story should take about five minutes. In three hundred seconds you want to get the children's attention and present the story in a way that will get a lesson across and be remembered. This book includes forty Old and New Testament stories. Each story has a short memory verse. You will find a list of suggested objects to be shown during the telling of the story. Also there is a brief introduction to set the scene. The Bible story itself is short and to the point. In some cases patterns are provided. These are located in the back of the book.

If time permits, you will find follow-up activities to reinforce each lesson. In addition, every story has a picture that may be used as an art project. These pictures may be saved and compiled into books by the children. They may be put together under different subjects, such as Old or New Testament, Bible heroes, miracles, Jesus, etc. Children will enjoy designing their own book covers, using construction paper, oilcloth, wallpaper samples, etc. The coloring pages may also be used as take-home papers for children to share with their families.

Every object in this book is meant to be a teaching tool. A container of mud will help children remember Jesus putting mud on the blind man's eyes. A hammer and saw will bring to life Noah building the boat. Pray for God's guidance as you share these Bible stories. Present them with enthusiasm and love, and your students will reap the blessings!

SS2875

TABLE OF CONTENTS

OLD TESTAMENT

SS2875

NEW TESTAMENT

GOD MADE IT ALL

"In the beginning God created the heavens and the earth."   Genesis 1:1

OBJECTS

Container of water
Container of dirt and rocks
Planted flower
Star, moon, and sun (patterns on page 85)
Animal figurine

INTRODUCTION

Place objects in a group on a table. As you remove each one in order, ask children to imagine a world without animals, stars, moon, sun, vegetation, land, or water. As you pick up each object, lead the children in discussing what they would be missing if any of these things no longer existed. When all the objects are removed, ask what is left. Explain that before time began there was only God, but He decided to create a wonderful new world.

BIBLE STORY

Read or tell in your own words the story on page 6. As an object is mentioned in the story replace it on the table.

FOLLOW-UP ACTIVITIES

1. **Coloring Book:** Reproduce for each child the picture and story on page 6. Prepare folders for the children. These may be purchased, or large sheets of paper may be folded in half. When a picture is colored, have the child place it in the folder. Refer to the Introduction on page 2 for suggested ways to compile coloring books.

2. **Mobile:** You'll need magazines, paper, glue, scissors, yarn, and coat hangers. Instruct children to select and cut pictures from magazines that show God's beautiful world. Have them glue pictures on large sheets of paper, making colorful collages. Cut out large circles from the collages. Providing different lengths of yarn, have children glue two circles back to back with a length of yarn in between. When dry attach several to a coat hanger. On a strip of paper print, "GOD MADE IT ALL," and secure it to the hanger. The star, moon, and sun patterns on page 85 may also be used to complete the mobile.

     SS2875

GOD MADE IT ALL
Genesis 1

Long ago there was no world. There was only darkness and God. Then God decided to make a very special place. On the first day of His labors He divided the darkness, making light that He called day and the dark He called night.

Next God commanded that there be a sky above which was filled with clean, fresh air. This was the second day. On the third day God formed the waters below the sky into great seas. Then He made dry ground appear and He called it land.

On the fourth day God did a wondrous thing. He made the land bring forth all kinds of vegetation: seed-bearing trees, fruits, bushes, flowers, green grass. This new world was becoming very beautiful! Next He looked up into the sky and He "decorated" it. In the night sky He put stars and a moon. In the day sky He placed a bright sun.

As the fifth day dawned God set about to put living things on His new world. He made fish for the seas. He made birds to fly in the sky.

On the sixth day God made the animals that walk upon the land and live in the forests and jungles He had created. Finally God decided His new world needed one more thing–people. God in His wisdom and love made man and woman. He gave to them the new world and all that was in it. It was theirs to care for.

On the seventh day God looked at all He had created and declared it was good. God blessed this day and called it holy. Then God rested.

THE SNEAKY SNAKE

"The woman said, 'The serpent deceived me, and I ate.'" Genesis 3:13b

OBJECTS

Small rubber snake (Instructions for making a
   snake are in the follow-up activities.)
An apple
Small paper bag

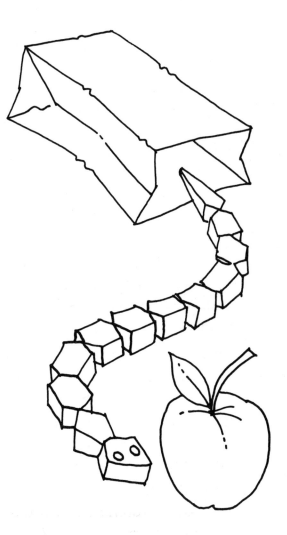

INTRODUCTION

Print in large letters on a chalkboard or paper the word "temptation." Ask children what this word means. Continue by asking them to share times when they have been tempted to do something they knew was wrong. Tell the class that today they will learn about two people in the Bible who were tempted and ended up in a whole lot of trouble!

BIBLE STORY

With the snake and apple in a paper bag, read or tell in your own words the story on page 8. Emphasize the *S* words to sound like the hissing of a snake. When the snake appears in the story, pull out the rubber snake from the bag. When the woman picks the fruit, remove the apple and take a bite. Repeat for the man.

FOLLOW-UP ACTIVITIES

1. **Coloring Book:** Reproduce the picture and story on page 8. Finished pictures may be filed in individual folders and later compiled into books.

2. **Egg Carton Snake:** You'll need the snake patterns on page 92, Styrofoam™ egg cartons, pipe cleaners, and construction paper.
Cut out six individual egg cups for each child. Help her connect the cups with short pieces of pipe cleaner. Reproduce the snake patterns for each child. Glue in place. Children may be challenged to have their snakes "speak," using only words that begin with *S*.

 SS2875

THE SNEAKY SNAKE

Genesis 3

God prepared a beautiful garden for the man and woman He had created. He told them they could eat any fruit except that which grew on the tree in the center of the garden. God warned them that the fruit of that tree would bring death.

One day a sneaky snake slithered into the garden. It silently slunk up into a swaying tree and settled down. The man and woman came walking by and the sneaky snake smiled and asked, "Did God really tell you that you could not eat any of the fruit?"

The woman replied, "We cannot eat from the tree in the middle of the garden. It is deadly!"

The sneaky snake snickered and said, "He's lying to you. He simply doesn't want you to be as smart as He is."

The woman thought for a moment, then picked a fruit from the tree and took a big bite. The sneaky snake smiled. The woman told the man to take a bite. He did! The sneaky snake was filled with supreme satisfaction.

Later God asked the man and woman what they had done. The man blamed the woman and the woman blamed the sneaky snake. God was angry. He told the sneaky snake that he would be forever hated. Then God sent the man and woman out of the beautiful garden and said they could never return.

SS2875

GOD'S BOATBUILDER

"Noah did everything just as God commanded him."   Genesis 6:22

OBJECTS

Hammer, saw, and nails
Piece of wood

INTRODUCTION

Place a table in front of the class. Ask how it was made. Talk about the materials needed to make the table. Ask what tools would be used to construct it. Mention that, as important as the right wood and proper tools are, there is one more thing that is more important. The table could not be made without a builder—a person who knows how to handle wood and use tools. Explain that you are going to tell a story about a man in the Bible who was asked by God to build something unusual and very big.

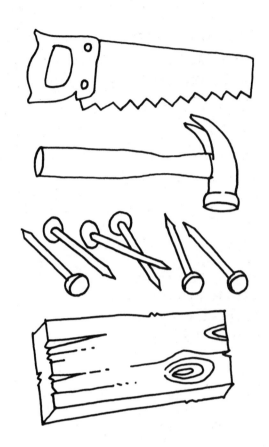

BIBLE STORY

Read or tell in your own words the story on page 10. As you begin to describe the building of the ark, show the class the hammer, saw, and nails. At this point, you may wish to actually saw a board or hammer nails into a piece of wood.

FOLLOW-UP ACTIVITIES

1. **Coloring Book:** Reproduce the picture and story on page 10. The finished pictures may be filed in individual folders and later compiled into books.

2. **God's Tools:** You'll need large sheets of paper and various tools (from a child's tool set would be best).
   Have each child choose a tool, place it on paper, and trace around it. When the papers are covered with tool outlines, have children print names of people in the Bible who were led by God to do difficult things. Noah should be their first choice. Others might include: Jesus, David, Gideon, Elijah, Moses, etc.

GOD'S BOATBUILDER
Genesis 6

When the man and woman disobeyed God, sin and death entered the world. God was very sad as He looked upon His creation and saw the wickedness. He felt He must destroy the evil world, but He found one good man and his name was Noah.

God told Noah He planned to send a great flood that would drown every living thing. He would save Noah and his family, but first Noah must build a huge ark. Noah did not hesitate. He listened carefully to God's instructions. Noah and his sons would saw the cypress wood and hammer it together to make the ark. And what an ark it would be—450 feet long, 75 feet wide, and 45 feet high! The boat would have three decks and many rooms, for God told Noah he must put two of every animal in the ark. There would also need to be space for their food. God had given Noah a tremendous task!

As Noah worked on the ark, people came by and laughed at him. They taunted him and called him crazy. They did not believe God would send a flood to cover the earth. Some said, "Noah is a fool." Still, Noah and his sons faithfully worked on the ark. When it was completed, the animals came two by two into the ark. Finally, Noah and his family entered, and God closed the door. Then the rain began to fall. Noah had done all God had asked of him. The great ark was soon floating on the waters that covered the earth.

SS2875

3 1833 02552 4551

A SIGN IN THE SKY

"I have set my rainbow in the clouds."   Genesis 9:13a

OBJECTS

Crayons or markers: red, orange, yellow, green,
  blue, indigo, and violet
Large sheet of paper

INTRODUCTION

Hold up each crayon. Ask children to name something in God's world that is each color. Ask them to
look around the room and find things that are these
seven colors. Explain that you are going to tell a
story from the Bible about something beautiful
that has all seven of these colors.

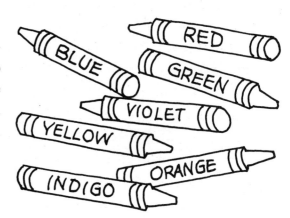

BIBLE STORY

Read or tell in your own words the story on page 12.
As you tell the story, draw a rainbow on the sheet of
paper. When the color red is mentioned, color a
narrow band of red in the shape of a half circle to
form the top of the rainbow. As each color appears
in the story, add that color to the rainbow.

FOLLOW-UP ACTIVITIES

1. **Coloring Book:** Reproduce the picture and story on page 12. The finished pictures
   may be filed in individual folders and later compiled into books.

2. **God's Rainbow:** You'll need the rainbow and cloud patterns on page 86, and yarn,
   glitter, small buttons, sequins, lace, ribbon, etc., in the seven colors of a rainbow as
   listed at the top of the page.
   Reproduce the rainbow and cloud patterns for each child. Let the children select
   from the materials to make rainbows, using the seven colors mentioned in the story.
   They will fill in each of the rainbow arcs in order, beginning with red and ending
   with violet. Show them how to cut out the two clouds and glue one at each end of
   the completed rainbow.

A SIGN IN THE SKY

Genesis 9

Noah and his family and all the animals had been safe in the ark just as God had promised. They had floated on the water for many days. Now God said they could come out onto the dry land.

Noah built an altar to the Lord and offered a sacrifice to Him. Then God made a promise to Noah and to all who would ever live on the earth. God said He would never send another flood to destroy the world. People could enjoy the red apples on the trees, the orange-striped tigers in the jungle, fields filled with yellow sunflowers, green and lush grass on the hillsides, blue raindrops to water the growing things of the earth, indigo and violet flowers of all kinds, without worrying that God would flood it all.

As a sign that He would forever keep His promise, God placed a rainbow in the sky. It would be a reminder of the covenant or promise He had made. Do you know from the story the seven colors God used to form His rainbow? Look for them the next time you see a rainbow sweeping across the sky!

SS2875

ABRAHAM IS TESTED

"And through your offspring all nations on earth will be blessed, because you have obeyed me."
                                                                            Genesis 22:18

OBJECTS

Knife
Several small tree branches
Lighted candle in a container

INTRODUCTION

Ask children if they take tests in school. Do they know why they must take these tests? Say that the teacher will know from their answers if they have learned the material. Explain that sometimes God tests His children to see if they truly love Him and are obedient. Tell the class you are going to share a story about a man who was given a very hard test by God. Ask them to listen carefully to discover if the man passed or failed God's test.

BIBLE STORY

Read or tell in your own words the story on page 14. Show the knife, wood, and fire as they are mentioned in the story.

FOLLOW-UP ACTIVITIES

1. **Coloring Book:** Reproduce the picture and story on page 14. The finished pictures may be filed in individual folders and later compiled into books.

2. **A Quick Test:** You'll need branches, marshmallows, a lighted candle, and paper. Do this activity outdoors. Seat the children in a circle and give each a tree branch. Clear a spot in the center of the circle for a fire. Ask questions from the Bible story: What was the name of Abraham's son? What did God command Abraham to do? What kind of offering was Abraham to give? If a child gives the correct answer, he may place a branch in the center of the circle. When all the branches are in a neat pile, light paper and start a fire to roast marshmallows, using other branches as sticks.

ABRAHAM IS TESTED

Genesis 22:1-18

God blessed Abraham by giving him a son in his old age. The boy's name was Isaac. One day God told Abraham to do a very difficult thing.

God said, "Take your son whom you love and go to Moriah. There you will sacrifice him as a burnt offering."

Abraham must have been filled with despair, but he obeyed. The next morning he gathered wood for the burnt offering. With Isaac and two of his servants, he set out for Moriah. They traveled for three days.

When they arrived, Abraham told the servants to wait while he and Isaac went to worship God. Isaac carried the wood and Abraham carried a container of fire and a knife.

Isaac was curious. He asked, "Father, we have the wood, the fire, and the knife for the offering, but where is the lamb?"

Abraham replied that God would provide the lamb.

Abraham built an altar and arranged the wood on it. He tied up Isaac and laid him on the altar on top of the wood. He raised the knife, but stopped when an angel of the Lord called to him.

The angel said, "Abraham, do not slay the boy, for now I know that you fear God."

Abraham looked up. Nearby a ram was caught by its horns in a thicket. Abraham released Isaac and offered the ram as a burnt sacrifice instead of his son. Would you say that Abraham passed or failed God's test?

JACOB'S DREAM

"Surely the Lord is in this place, and I was not aware of it."   Genesis 28:16b

OBJECTS

Large stone
Stairway and angels (patterns on page 87)
9" x 12" piece of flannel
8" x 10" piece of cardboard
Sheet of sandpaper

INTRODUCTION

Before class, cover the cardboard with flannel and glue or tape it in place. Reproduce the stairway and angel patterns. Glue small pieces of sandpaper on the back of the stairway and each angel.

Print the word "dream" on the chalkboard or on a piece of paper. Ask children if they dream when they sleep. Explain that dreams can be enjoyable, but sometimes they are bad. Then we call them nightmares. Today you are telling a story about a man who had a dream that changed his life. It began with a large stone. (Show the stone.)

BIBLE STORY

Read or tell in your own words the story on page 16. Show the stone again when it is mentioned. While describing the stairway and angels, mount those you have made on the flannel-covered cardboard.

FOLLOW-UP ACTIVITIES

1. **Coloring Book:** Reproduce the picture and story on page 16. The finished pictures may be filed in individual folders and later compiled into books.

2. **Mobile:** You'll need the patterns on page 87, sandpaper, flannel, cardboard, and glue.
   Reproduce the angel and stairway patterns for each child. Provide flannel and cardboard to make individual flannel boards. Instruct children to color and cut out the angels and stairway. Have them glue small sandpaper squares on each. Children may like to take turns telling the story of Jacob's dream, using their flannel boards.

JACOB'S DREAM
Genesis 28:10-22

Jacob was the son of Isaac and Rebekah. He displeased his father and brother, and was sent away to live with other relatives. It was a sad journey for Jacob. He stopped for the night in a stony place. He took one large stone, put it under his head for a pillow, and went to sleep. That must have been uncomfortable!

During the night, Jacob had a dream. He saw a stairway that reached from earth to heaven. On the stairway were angels going up and down. Then a marvelous thing happened. God appeared and spoke to Jacob. He gave Jacob the same promise He had given to Abraham and Isaac. Jacob's offspring would live in the Promised Land.

Jacob awoke and declared, "The Lord is surely in this place." Early the next morning he took the stone that had been his pillow and poured oil on it. In this way, he anointed the spot and called it Bethel. He made a vow that he would serve the Lord from that day on. A dream had changed Jacob's life forever.

 SS2875

A SPECIAL ROBE

"Now Israel loved Joseph more than any of his other sons."   Genesis 37:3a

OBJECTS
Child's coat or robe

INTRODUCTION
Ask children if they enjoy receiving gifts from their parents. Ask how would they feel if a brother or sister were given a beautiful new coat but they did not get one. (Show the coat.) Would they be jealous? How does God want us to respond when we have jealous feelings? Explain that today's Bible story is about someone who suffered because of others' jealousy.

BIBLE STORY
Read or tell in your own words the story on page 18. Ask one of the children to help you. When the robe is mentioned in the story, put the coat or robe on the child and give him a big hug. Take off the robe when the brothers remove Joseph's robe.

FOLLOW-UP ACTIVITIES

1. **Coloring Book:** Reproduce the picture and story on page 18. The finished pictures may be filed in individual folders and later compiled into books.

2. **Joseph's Robe:** You'll need the patterns on page 88, sequins, rickrack, cloth, and glue.
   Reproduce the patterns for each child. Provide craft supplies to decorate the robe. Instruct children to cut out Joseph and his robe, then glue the robe to the Joseph figure.

     SS2875

A SPECIAL ROBE
Genesis 37

Jacob had many sons, but his favorite was Joseph. To show his great love, Jacob gave Joseph a beautifully decorated robe. This made Joseph's brothers angry and jealous.

Young Joseph made things worse by tattling on his brothers and telling them about dreams that meant one day they would all bow down to him. The brothers hated Joseph and could not say a kind word to him.

One day Jacob sent Joseph to check on his brothers who were herding sheep. When the brothers saw Joseph coming, they plotted to kill him. Reuben suggested they just throw him into a cistern and leave him. He planned to come back later and rescue Joseph.

The brothers did as Reuben suggested, but first they took the despised robe off Joseph. As they sat nearby eating, a caravan on its way to Egypt approached. The brothers decided to sell Joseph to the travelers for twenty shekels of silver.

The brothers dipped Joseph's robe in the blood of a slain goat. They went home and told their father that Joseph had been killed by an animal. Jacob tore his clothes and wept. No one could comfort him. His favorite son was dead.

In Egypt, Joseph was a slave, but God was with him. Years later Joseph's brothers came to Egypt and Joseph forgave them for their jealous actions.

SS2875

WATER, WATER EVERYWHERE

"She named him Moses, saying, 'I drew him out of the water.'" Exodus 2:10b

OBJECTS

Five 3" x 5" cards
Five baby food jars

INTRODUCTION

Before class, fold the cards in half. Print on one side of each card a letter from the word "water." On the opposite side print a letter from the word "Moses." Fill the baby food jars with water.
Show the class one jar of water. Ask how many ways they use water. Say that you have a Bible story about a man that seemed to be always in water, around water, or doing something with water.

BIBLE STORY

Read or tell in your own words the story on page 20. Place the water cards in order in front of the jars as each water incident is told. When complete ask the children if they know the name of the man who spent so much time in water. Say that even his name means "water." Turn around each card to reveal the name "Moses."

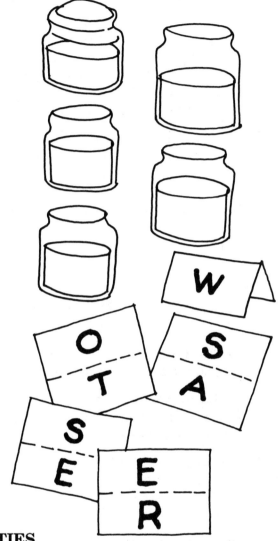

FOLLOW-UP ACTIVITIES

1. **Coloring Book:** Reproduce the picture and story on page 20. The finished pictures may be filed in individual folders and later compiled into books.

2. **Water Weight:** You'll need baby food jars, water, artificial flowers, and glitter.
Give each child a jar and a flower. Help each to put the flower inside the jar, then fill it with water. Add glitter. The lids may be painted or covered with cloth. Encourage children to give the water weights as gifts.

SS2875

WATER, WATER EVERYWHERE
Exodus 2; 7:16-24; 14; 17:1-8

This is the story of a man who always seems to be in or near water.

1. When this baby was born, his mother put him in a papyrus basket and hid him in the reeds along the bank of the Nile River to keep him from being killed. The daughter of Pharaoh found him and took him to her palace.

2. He grew up in the palace, but when Pharaoh became angry with him, he went to Midian. In Midian, he sat down by a well. Seven women came by to water their flocks. Some shepherds tried to drive them away, but he went to their rescue.

3. Eventually God commanded the man to return to Egypt and tell Pharaoh to let the Hebrews leave the country. God sent plagues upon the Egyptians to make Pharaoh cooperate. At one point, God told the man to strike the Nile River with his staff and it was changed to blood.

4. The man led the Hebrews out of Egypt, but the Pharaoh chased them with his army, trapping them at the Red Sea. God told the man to stretch his hand out over the sea, and it was divided so the people could cross over to safety. Pharaoh's army drowned.

5. The man led the Hebrews into the desert. They became thirsty and demanded that the man help them. God told him to strike a rock and water flowed out! Soon the people were drinking their fill.

Do you know the name of the man who found water everywhere he went?

Shining Star Publications, Copyright © 1993   SS2875

GOD'S RULES

"And God spoke all these words." Exodus 20:1

OBJECTS
Two 9" x 12" pieces of poster board or cardboard
Typing paper

INTRODUCTION
Before class, cut out fifteen 2" x 8" strips of paper. On ten, print commandments as found on the pattern on page 92. Print the following on the five remaining strips: You shall not eat candy on Sunday, You shall not talk loudly in church, You shall not drink sodas, You shall take care of your pets, You shall not ride your bike at night.

Ask children to share some of the rules they have to obey each day at home, school, or in the community. Explain that God gave His people some special rules to live by. Ask children to read the rules on the strips they have. As they listen carefully to the story, raise their hands if they hear their rules mentioned.

BIBLE STORY
Read or tell in your own words the story on page 22. When a child says she hears her rule, take the strip and tape it to the poster board. Place five commandments on each board. Have children read the five remaining rules and discuss why they are not from God.

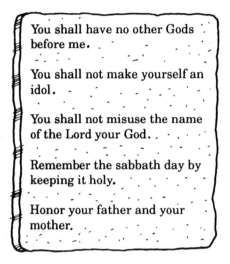

You shall have no other Gods before me.

You shall not make yourself an idol.

You shall not misuse the name of the Lord your God.

Remember the sabbath day by keeping it holy.

Honor your father and your mother.

You shall not murder.

You shall not commit adultery.

You shall not steal.

You shall not give false testimony.

You shall not covet.

FOLLOW-UP ACTIVITIES

1. **Coloring Book:** Reproduce the picture and story on page 22. The finished pictures may be filed in individual folders and later compiled into books.

2. **Ten Commandments:** You'll need clay, paper, glue, and the commandments pattern on page 92.
   Provide each child with enough clay to form two 3" x 5" "stone" tablets. Reproduce the commandments pattern for each child. Have the children glue the papers on the clay.

                                                                                           SS2875

GOD'S RULES
Exodus 20

Moses had led the Hebrew people out of Egyptian slavery. Now they were camped at Mount Sinai. God told Moses to meet him at the top of the mountain. Moses obeyed, and heard these commands from God:

1. The people were to have no other gods but Him.
2. They were not to make any idols to worship because God was a jealous God.
3. The people were not to use God's name in a bad way.
4. They were to keep the Sabbath day holy because it was the day God rested after creating the world.
5. God expected the people to honor their mothers and fathers. If they would do this, they would live long lives.
6. God's people should not murder.
7. He did not want them to commit adultery.
8. He did not want them to steal.
9. They should not tell lies about their neighbors.
10. They should not covet anything belonging to their neighbors.

All God's rules were written on stone tablets to be kept in a safe place from that day forward.

SS2875

THE WALLS COME DOWN

"Then the Lord said to Joshua, 'See, I have delivered Jericho into your hands, along with its king and its fighting men.'"

Joshua 6:2

OBJECTS

Children's building blocks
Toy horn

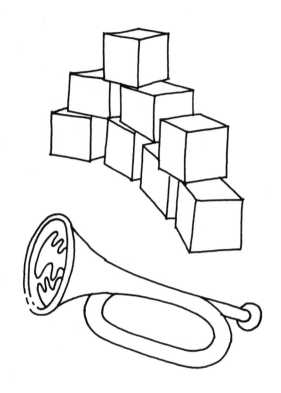

INTRODUCTION

On a table build a "wall" with blocks. Ask children: Why do people have walls around their homes? Why are there walls around a prison? What could bring these walls down? (armored tanks, earthquakes, dynamite, etc.) Explain that you are going to tell them a Bible story about a wall that came tumbling down because of faith.

BIBLE STORY

Read or tell in your own words the story on page 24. Blow the toy horn when this action is mentioned. Knock the "wall" down when the walls of Jericho come down.

FOLLOW-UP ACTIVITIES

1. **Coloring Book:** Reproduce the picture and story on page 24. The finished pictures can be filed in individual folders and later compiled into books.

2. **Words on a Wall:** You'll need construction paper and glue.
   On construction paper draw sixteen 1" x 2" "stones". On the stones print in scrambled order God's words from the memory verse: "See I have delivered Jericho into your hands, along with its king and its fighting men." Give each child a copy of the page and have him cut out the stones. Then have each child glue the cutout stones, with the words in the correct order, on another piece of paper, forming a wall. The wall may be built with two rows of eight stones or four rows of four each.

THE WALLS COME DOWN
Joshua 6:1-20

Joshua had become the leader of the Hebrew people. The precious Ten Commandments had been placed in a box called the ark of the covenant. It was time for the people to go into the land that God had promised them, but obstacles stood in their way. One of these was the great walled city of Jericho.

The walls of Jericho were so thick that houses were built on top of them. The Hebrews must have wondered how they would be able to take this city, but God had a plan which He told Joshua. The armed men were to march around Jericho once a day for six days. They walked in front of and behind seven priests carrying the ark of the covenant and trumpets. The priests blew the trumpets as they marched. The inhabitants of Jericho must have stood on their great walls laughing at the strange Hebrews. No one could take their city this way!

On the seventh day, God told Joshua to have the priests march around the walls of Jericho seven times, blowing their trumpets. The people of Jericho must have been very puzzled by these invaders. As the Hebrews started around the walls for the seventh time, the priests gave one long blast on their trumpets. For the first time, all the Hebrew people gave a great shout. The strong, thick walls of Jericho collapsed to the ground! Joshua and his armed men rushed across the rubble and took the city of Jericho. God had given them a great victory! The walls had come down!

SS2875

GIDEON, THE GENERAL

"Grasping the torches in their left hands and holding in their right hands the trumpets they were to blow, they shouted, 'A sword for the Lord and for Gideon!'"

Judges 7:20b

OBJECTS

Toy horn
Flashlight
Paper bag

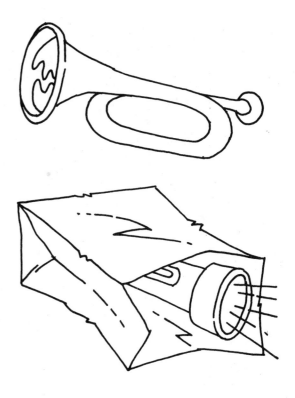

INTRODUCTION

Place the horn and flashlight on a table. Ask children: What kind of weapons do soldiers use in a battle (tanks, guns, planes, bombs)? What did they use in Bible times (swords, spears, bows, and arrows)? Explain that you will tell them a Bible story about a battle that used a trumpet and a light. (Hold up both objects, then put the flashlight in the bag.)

BIBLE STORY

Read or tell in your own words the story on page 26. Show the horn and the bag with the light when mentioned. At the appropriate time blow the horn and bring out the turned-on flashlight from the bag.

FOLLOW-UP ACTIVITIES

1. **Coloring Book:** Reproduce the picture and story on page 26. The finished pictures may be filed in individual folders and later compiled into books.

2. **Matching Game:** You'll need the trumpet and jar patterns on page 93 and paper. Cut out five trumpets and five jars from the patterns. On the trumpets print: Gideon, angel, Midianites, water, and three hundred. On the jars print: general, messenger, enemy, drink, and God's army. Mix up the trumpets and jars and place them on a table or bulletin board. Have children match each trumpet with a jar. You may prefer to scatter the trumpets and jars around the room and have five children look for the trumpets and five others look for the jars. Then each child may find the person who has the trumpet or jar that matches his.

GIDEON, THE GENERAL

Judges 6:11-16; 7:1-22

The people of Israel had turned to wickedness and were being oppressed by the Midianites. God selected a farmer named Gideon to lead the Israelites.

God sent His angel to Gideon with a message. The angel called Gideon a mighty warrior whom God would help to fight the Midianites. Gideon could hardly believe his ears! He was not a military leader, but he obeyed God's call.

Gideon sent word to the people that he needed an army. Thirty–two thousand men arrived. God looked at the army and told Gideon it was too large! God said any who were afraid could go home. Twenty–two thousand immediately left. Now there were ten thousand. God said there were still too many! He told Gideon to watch the men as they went to the water for a drink. God wanted only those who drank the water from their hands and kept their weapons nearby. Only three hundred did. God's army was now ready.

God gave Gideon an unusual battle plan. He told him to divide the army into three groups of one hundred each, give each soldier a trumpet and a jar with a lighted torch inside, then have the whole army surround the Midianite camp while they slept.

Gideon did as God said. At the signal, the soldiers blew their trumpets and smashed the jars. With the trumpet in one hand and the torch in the other, each man shouted and blew his trumpet again. The Midianites awoke and were terrified. They thought a great army was attacking! They began running everywhere. In a short time Gideon and his army defeated the Midianites!

SS2875

SO GREAT A LOVE

"Where you go I will go, and where you stay I will stay. Your people will be my people and your God my God."   Ruth 1:16b

OBJECTS
Three paper hearts (pattern on page 96)
A sandal

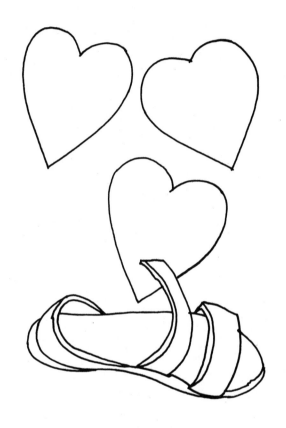

INTRODUCTION
Before class, cut out three red paper hearts. Print "Ruth, Boaz, and God" on them.
Begin by holding up the sandal. Explain that in Bible times when a man sold a piece of property, one man would take off his sandal and give it to the other. This made the sale legal! (Hold up the hearts with the names Ruth and Boaz on them.) Say: Here's a Bible story about a woman named Ruth and a man named Boaz who took off his sandal to show his love.

BIBLE STORY
Read or tell in your own words the story on page 28. Hold up the Ruth and Boaz hearts and the sandal when they are mentioned. Near the end of the story, secure the two hearts to a bulletin board or wall leaving a space between them. At the conclusion, place the God heart between the Ruth and Boaz hearts.

FOLLOW-UP ACTIVITIES

1. **Coloring Book:** Reproduce the picture and story on page 28. The finished pictures may be filed in individual folders and later compiled into books.

2. **Heart to Heart:** You'll need construction paper, glue, and the heart pattern on page 96.
   Fold the sheets of paper into fourths like a greeting card. Using the pattern, cut out red hearts and give two to each child. Instruct children to print "You" on one and "God" on the other. On the outside of the folded paper, print in large letters "Good News Inside." Have children glue the God heart on the inside left and the You heart on the right side. At the top between the two hearts they should print the word "Loves." Suggest that they give the cards to people who do not attend church or to those who need cheering up.

SO GREAT A LOVE
Ruth 1-4

Boaz was a rich farmer. One day he was visiting one of his fields when he saw a young woman he did not recognize. He asked one of his harvesters who she was. The man said, "She is Ruth. She came from Moab with her mother-in-law, Naomi."

Boaz was even more interested because Naomi was a relative of his. The harvester continued, "Ruth is a hard worker. She has been gleaning since early morning without stop. I know her work keeps food on the table for her and Naomi."

Boaz was impressed with the beautiful and kind woman. He told her to come to his fields every day and he told his harvesters to always leave extra wheat for her.

Ruth told Naomi all about Boaz. Naomi knew him to be a good man. She wanted Ruth to have a home. Boaz would make her an excellent husband!

As the days passed, Ruth and Boaz realized they were in love. Boaz wanted to marry Ruth, but the law said she could only marry her closest relative and that was not Boaz. Boaz decided to meet the man at the town gate and discuss the matter. Ruth must have been very anxious to hear what happened at that meeting.

When Boaz came to her he had good news. The relative had agreed to sell all his rights. Boaz had removed his sandal and made the sale legal. Ruth and Boaz were soon married and Naomi came to live with them. In time Ruth had a son. He was named Obed.

Ruth and Boaz loved each other deeply, but most of all they showed by their actions that they had an even greater love for God.

 SS2875

A CALL FROM GOD

"Then Samuel said, 'Speak, for your servant is listening.' "
1 Samuel 3:10b

OBJECTS
Two toy telephones

INTRODUCTION
Give a phone to one of the children. Using the second phone, call the child up and talk about attending some church activity. When the conversation is over, place both phones on a table. Say that because of phones people in faraway lands can call and talk to people around the world. In Bible times there were no phones, but once a young boy received a very special call that was straight from heaven!

BIBLE STORY
Read or tell in your own words the story on page 30. Speak into one phone when God calls. Speak into the second phone when Samuel answers.

FOLLOW-UP ACTIVITIES

1. **Coloring Book:** Reproduce the picture and story on page 30. The finished pictures may be filed in individual folders and later compiled into books.

2. **Telephone Fun:** You'll need Styrofoam™ cups or tin cans, string, and a small screwdriver.
   Punch a hole in the bottom of each cup or can with the screwdriver. Help children insert the ends of a six-foot length of string into the cups or cans. Have pairs of children speak through their "phones." Suggest conversations you would like them to have: call someone who is sick, call a person you have hurt to apologize, ask a friend to come to church, call a Bible character (Jonah, Moses, Peter, Daniel, etc.) and talk about his adventures. Suggest that children go home and call someone who would enjoy hearing from them: a shut-in, older relative, sick person, lonely neighbor, etc.

SS2875

A CALL FROM GOD

1 Samuel 3

Long ago the house of the Lord was in a place called Shiloh. Eli was the priest who cared for it. A woman named Hannah had promised if she ever had a child she would bring him to the Holy Place to serve God and help Eli. Hannah soon had a son named Samuel. The boy came to live with Eli. Samuel was a great joy to the elderly priest. His own sons were wicked and made Eli very sad.

One night when Eli and Samuel were asleep, Samuel heard a voice calling him. "Samuel!" The boy thought it was Eli. He ran to Eli saying, "Here I am." The priest said he had not called Samuel and told him to lie back down. Samuel obeyed.

Shortly, Samuel heard the voice again saying, "Samuel!" For the second time Samuel rushed to Eli. Again the priest said he had not called him.

For a third time the boy heard someone call, "Samuel!" He again ran to Eli. The priest realized that this must be God calling Samuel. He told the boy, "Go and lie down. If the voice calls again, speak to Him."

As Samuel lay there, God called, "Samuel! Samuel!" Samuel said, "Speak, for your servant is listening."

The Lord told Samuel that Eli's wicked sons were going to be punished. The next morning, the priest insisted that Samuel tell him what God had said. Samuel told Eli everything.

SS2875

A SHEPHERD BECOMES KING

"Then the Lord said, 'Rise and anoint him; he is the one.' " 1 Samuel 16:12b

OBJECTS

Crook (wooden stick)
Harp (autoharp)
Slingshot (child's toy)
Crown (made of paper)
   (Or use the patterns on page 89)

INTRODUCTION

If you're using the patterns, before class color and glue the figures on heavy paper and cut them out.

Stand before the class with the crown on your head, the crook and harp in one hand, and the slingshot in the other. Explain that in the Bible there was a man who was very talented. He was a shepherd (show the crook), a songwriter (show the harp), a soldier (show slingshot), and a king (show the crown). Tell the children to listen carefully to the story and learn who this shepherd, songwriter, soldier, king was.

BIBLE STORY

Read or tell in your own words the story on page 32. Show the crook, harp, slingshot, and crown when mentioned.

FOLLOW-UP ACTIVITIES

1. **Coloring Book:** Reproduce the picture and story on page 32. The finished pictures may be filed in individual folders and later compiled into books.

2. **"David Did It" Game:** You'll need the patterns on page 89, paper, and glue. Reproduce the patterns for each child to color and cut out. With the children seated on the floor, have them put the cutouts in front of them. Give a clue about David or another Bible person. Tell the children to hold up a cutout if the clue is about David and what he did. (Examples: He killed a giant. He was anointed by Samuel. He sang and wrote psalms. He cared for his father's sheep. He was put in a lions' den. He fought the Midianites with trumpets and pitchers. He was married to Queen Esther.) Children may glue the cutouts on paper with "David" printed at the top of the page.

A SHEPHERD BECOMES KING

1 Samuel 16-17

Samuel was sent by God to find a new king for the people of Israel. Saul had been chosen, but he had displeased God. Samuel journeyed to Bethlehem to the home of Jesse, who had several sons.

Jesse's seven sons were all rejected by God. Samuel asked Jesse if he had any other sons. Jesse replied that the youngest, David, was out tending the sheep. Samuel sent for David. When he entered, the Lord told Samuel, "Rise and anoint him; he is the one." Israel had a new king! But David was very young and not ready to become a king. He had much to learn, and Saul was still in charge.

Saul was tormented by evil spirits. He asked his attendants to find someone who could play a harp. The person they brought was David, who often sang and played as he watched the sheep. David's harp music soothed the troubled ruler.

Soon after that, Saul's army was at war with the Philistines. The enemy had a champion named Goliath who was over nine feet tall! No one in Saul's army dared fight him. Three of Jesse's sons were in the army, so he sent David to check on them. When David heard Goliath's challenge to fight, he volunteered! Saul wanted him to wear heavy armor, but David said that with God's help he only needed his slingshot. He had used it to protect his sheep from lions and wolves. David went out to meet Goliath. The giant laughed at him, but David whirled the slingshot around his head and shot a stone that sent Goliath to the ground. With God's help, David had defeated the great giant.

SS2875

GOD PROVIDES

"For the jar of flour was not used up and the jug of oil did not run dry, in keeping with the word of the Lord spoken by Elijah."   1 Kings 17:16

OBJECTS
Containers of vegetable oil and flour
Bowl and spoon
Precooked cake (recipe under follow-up activities)

INTRODUCTION
Ask the class to mention things which they know God provides for them (sunshine, rain, food, etc.). Ask if they can imagine what life would be like without the things God provides. Explain that without sunshine and rain, crops would not grow and there could not be the food we expect to eat each day. In Bible times such an event occurred. The rain did not come, and the people soon ran out of food. God intervened to help a prophet, a widow, and her young son.

BIBLE STORY
Read or tell in your own words the story on page 34. As you talk about the flour and oil, pour small portions into the bowl and mix together. Show the cake when the widow gives a piece to Elijah.

FOLLOW-UP ACTIVITIES
1. **Coloring Book:** Reproduce the picture and story on page 34. The finished pictures may be filed in individual folders and later compiled into books.

2. **Making an Elijah Cake:** You'll need flour, oil, egg, milk, utensils, and an electric griddle.
   Take your class to a kitchen or bring an electric griddle. Beat together $1\frac{1}{4}$ cups of sifted flour, 1 egg, $\frac{3}{4}$ cup milk, and 3 tablespoons oil until smooth. Drop by spoonfuls onto a hot, oiled griddle. Cook on one side until full of bubbles. Turn and cook the other side. Serve to the children while warm. (This recipe makes eleven 4" cakes.) Be sure to say grace, thanking God for the food He provides each day. Remind children how glad Elijah, the widow, and her son were to have a simple cake to eat everyday.

GOD PROVIDES

1 Kings 17:8-16

Elijah had prophesied that it would not rain for a long time. King Ahab was angered by Elijah's words, so God told Elijah to leave. God said He would watch over Elijah. He sent him to the town of Zarephath in Sidon.

As Elijah was going through the town gate, he saw a widow gathering sticks. He was thirsty from his journey, and asked her to get him a drink. He also asked for a piece of bread. The widow sadly replied that she was gathering sticks to build a fire to make one last cake for her and her son. She had only a little flour and a little oil left. When it was gone she and her son would die.

Elijah said to her, "Don't be afraid. Go home and do as you have said. But first make a small cake of bread for me from what you have and bring it to me, and then make something for yourself and your son."

The widow easily could have told Elijah to get lost! Elijah told her if she would feed him, God would keep her jar of flour and jug of oil full until the rains came again.

The widow went to her home and did as Elijah had said. She made a cake for Elijah and brought it to him. Then she prepared two cakes for herself and her son. From that day on, her jar of flour and jug of oil were never empty. God had provided just as Elijah knew He would!

SS2875

MOUNT CARMEL CONTEST

"Then the fire of the Lord fell and burned up the sacrifice, the wood, the stones and the soil, and also licked up the water in the trench."   I Kings 18:38

OBJECTS

Container of water
Small sticks
Matches
Nonflammable container

INTRODUCTION

Show children the sticks and matches. Ask if they have ever been on a camping trip. When they gather wood for the fire, do they look for wet sticks or dry ones? Why do they need dry sticks? Place sticks in the nonflammable container, pour on the water, and try to light the sticks with matches. Explain that you are going to tell a Bible story about a man who had to face 450 men in a contest that included water, wood, and fire. Children should listen carefully to see what happened.

BIBLE STORY

Read or tell in your own words the story on page 36. Show the sticks, water, and matches (fire) when mentioned.

FOLLOW-UP ACTIVITIES

1. **Coloring Book:** Reproduce the picture and story on page 36. The finished pictures may be filed in individual folders and later compiled into books.

2. **Pick Up the Sticks:** You'll need twelve craft sticks and an ink pen.
   On each craft stick print one of these words: Elijah, Ahab, God, Baal, shout, pray, fire, water, good, evil, faith, unbelief. Put the sticks in a pile on a table or floor. Let children take turns picking up a stick without making any others move. When all the sticks are picked up, have each child find the person with the stick that says the opposite of his.

MOUNT CARMEL CONTEST
1 Kings 18:16-39

The rain did not come to the land of Israel, just as the Prophet Elijah had said. Then God told Elijah to go to Ahab with a challenge. Elijah told Ahab to have all the Israelite people come to Mount Carmel. There he would face the prophets of Baal in a contest to see whose God was stronger. Ahab agreed.

On the day of the contest, 450 prophets of Baal climbed up the mountain. Elijah stood waiting for them. The people gathered around. Elijah told the people they could no longer serve two gods. They must choose between God or Baal.

Elijah asked for two bulls. He told the prophets of Baal to cut theirs up and place it on the wood but not set it on fire. They must ask Baal to start the fire. Elijah said he would do the same when it was his turn.

The 450 prophets prepared the bull and the wood. Then they began to shout as loudly as they could for Baal to answer them and set the wood on fire. They did this for hours, but the wood did not burn. Elijah suggested that they shout louder. They did, but still no answer. The 450 prophets finally gave up; then it was Elijah's turn.

He gathered twelve stones and made an altar. He put the wood on top with the cut up bull on it. He dug a ditch around the altar, then ordered that four jars of water be poured on the sacrifice! He did this three times until the water poured down and filled the ditch. Then Elijah prayed to God, asking Him to show His great power. God sent down fire that burned up the wood, bull, stones, and water! The people began to cry, "The Lord—He is God! The Lord—He is God!" The Mount Carmel contest was over!

NAAMAN IS HEALED

"He stood before him and said, 'Now I know that there is no God in all the world except in Israel. . . .'"   2 Kings 5:15b

OBJECTS
Small pad of stick-on notes

INTRODUCTION
Ask children if they have ever had or known someone who has had chicken pox. Discuss the itchy sores it causes. Explain that in Bible times there was a terrible skin disease called leprosy. Chicken pox is uncomfortable, but soon goes away. Leprosy, in time, can destroy the whole body. This is what was going to happen to a man named Naaman until he met a prophet of God.

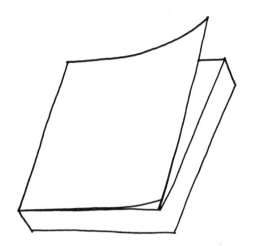

BIBLE STORY
Read or tell in your own words the story on page 38. When telling about Naaman's leprosy, begin putting stick-on notes on your face, hands, arms, legs, etc. Begin removing them when Naaman goes into the Jordan River. Have them all removed when he is cleansed.

FOLLOW-UP ACTIVITIES

1. **Coloring Book:** Reproduce the picture and story on page 38. The finished pictures may be filed in individual folders and later compiled into books.

2. **Stick-on Scramble:** You'll need a small pad of stick-on notes.
   Print the letters from these words on stick-on notes: Naaman, leprosy, Elisha, Jordan, and seven. Have five children come forward. Stick on the first child the letters of "Naaman" in any order (stick them in order for younger children). Stick "leprosy" letters on the second child, etc. Ask questions, and have children point to the child who has the answer stuck on him. 1. Who was the commander of a great army? 2. What terrible disease did this man have? 3. Whom did a captive Israelite girl say the commander should go see? 4. In what river did the man tell the commander to wash? 5. How many times was the commander to wash himself? When a correct choice is made, the child with the stick-ons can remove them and stick them in the right order on a wall, table, or poster board.

NAAMAN IS HEALED
2 Kings 5:1-16

A young girl from Israel had been carried off to Aram as a slave. She served the wife of Naaman, commander of the army. Naaman was a great man, but he had a terrible disease called leprosy. His body was covered with large sores. The Israelite girl was kind, and she told Naaman about a prophet in Samaria who could cure his leprosy. This man of God was named Elisha.

Naaman rode to Samaria in a chariot and brought many servants and gifts. He was an important visitor, but Elisha did not come out to greet him! Instead, Elisha sent a messenger to say that Naaman should wash himself seven times in the Jordan River. Naaman was furious! How dare this prophet treat him in such an unfriendly way. Naaman had expected Elisha to wave his hand over him and the leprosy would be gone. He turned to go home. Naaman's servants came and said to him, "If Elisha had told you to do some hard thing like pull your chariot up a high mountain, you would have done it. Why not at least try this simple thing and see if it works?"

Naaman listened to his servants, and went down into the Jordan River. He washed once, then twice. He noticed that some sores were getting smaller! He went in a third and fourth time. Now some were even disappearing. Naaman washed a fifth and sixth time. His skin was almost clear. When he came out of the water the seventh time, the leprosy was gone! Naaman declared that there was no God in all the world except in Israel!

SS2875

A BIBLE BURNER

"The king cut them off with a scribe's knife and threw them into the firepot, until the entire scroll was burned in the fire."   Jeremiah 36:23b

OBJECTS

Nonflammable container
Two small scrolls
Scissors
Matches

INTRODUCTION

Before class, make the scrolls by rolling the ends of sheets of paper toward each other. These may be secured with a string.

Show one scroll to your class and say: This is the way the Bible was written long ago. A person had to take a sheet of paper and pen and ink and write every word. It was hard work, so the words of God were very precious. Once there was a king who did not think that God's Word was special.

BIBLE STORY

Read or tell in your own words the story on page 40. When the scroll is burned, cut up the small scroll with the scissors, place it in the nonflammable container, and set it on fire with a match. Show the second scroll when it is mentioned in the story.

FOLLOW-UP ACTIVITIES

1. **Coloring Book:** Reproduce the picture and story on page 40. The finished pictures may be filed in individual folders and later compiled into books.

2. **Scroll Verses:** You'll need 4" x 6" sheets of paper, string, and optional dowels or pencils.
   Give the children sheets of paper. Have them print out selected Bible verses. These may be verses related to God's Word: Psalm 119:105; Luke 24:27; John 5:39; Romans 15:4. Other subjects may also be used: love, courage, kindness, etc. Children may roll the ends of paper toward each other and secure them with string. Two pencils or dowels may be glued to the ends of the paper, then rolled together and secured. Emphasize that it is important to learn God's Word. We want it to stay in our hearts and minds forever.

                    SS2875

A BIBLE BURNER
Jeremiah 36

When King Jehoiakim ruled Judah, God spoke to his prophet Jeremiah. He told Jeremiah to write down all the words He had spoken to him. God wanted to remind people what would happen if they continued in their wicked ways.

Jeremiah knew it would be a great task to put all God's words on paper. He called for Baruch to help him. While Jeremiah spoke the words, Baruch wrote them on the scroll. When the scroll was done, Jeremiah sent Baruch to the Lord's temple to read the words to all the people there.

Some officials heard the reading, and were filled with great fear. They felt the king should know about these words.

The scroll was brought to King Jehoiakim and read by Jehudi. It was wintertime and the king had a fire burning in the pot in front of him. As Jehudi read from the scroll, the king took a knife and cut off pieces of it and threw them into the fire. He did not want to hear that God would punish Judah for its disobedience. When he finished burning the scroll, he told the officials to arrest Baruch and Jeremiah, but God had hidden them.

God told Jeremiah and Baruch to write the scroll one more time. He said that King Jehoiakim would be punished for burning the first scroll. So once again, Jeremiah spoke God's words and Baruch wrote them down.

SS2875

FAITHFUL DANIEL

"My God sent his angel, and he shut the mouths of the lions. They have not hurt me, because I was found innocent in his sight."   Daniel 6:22a

OBJECTS
Finger puppets—Daniel, Darius, lions, and
  angel (patterns on page 90)
Bowl of fruit
Bowl of sugared doughnuts

INTRODUCTION
Before class, reproduce the finger puppet patterns, cut them out, and glue the ends together.

Place the fruit and doughnuts on a table. Explain that sometimes we have to choose what is best for us. Ask: Which of these foods would you rather eat? Which do you think is better for you? Explain that when the prophet Daniel was a boy, he made this kind of choice. He chose to eat food that he knew pleased God. Then Daniel became a man and had to make an even harder choice.

BIBLE STORY
Read or tell in your own words the story on page 42. When Daniel is mentioned, place his puppet on your index finger. When Darius is mentioned, place his puppet on your thumb. When Daniel is put in the lions' den, put the three lions on your remaining fingers. Remove Darius and replace him with the angel when the angel appears. At the end of story, remove the lions and angel, leaving only Daniel.

FOLLOW-UP ACTIVITIES

1. **Coloring Book:** Reproduce the picture and story on page 42. The finished pictures may be filed in individual folders and later compiled into books.

2. **Finger Puppet Fun:** You'll need the patterns on page 90, paper, and tape or glue. Reproduce the patterns for each child. Have children color, cut out, and tape or glue the ends together to fit their fingers. Then let them act out the story of Faithful Daniel.

SS2875

FAITHFUL DANIEL
Daniel 6

Daniel was a boy when he was captured and taken to Babylon, but he was faithful to God. He declared he would not eat any food that had been offered to an idol. Daniel grew strong and wise and became a powerful man in Babylon.

Darius was king. He liked Daniel but others were jealous and wanted to kill him. They asked Darius to make a decree that for thirty days no one could pray to any other god but the king. If they disobeyed, they would be killed by lions. (The men knew that Daniel prayed three times a day to his God.) Vain Darius agreed.

Daniel knew about the decree, and knew if he prayed he could die. This did not stop faithful Daniel. He prayed as he always had, and the evil men rushed to tell King Darius. The sad king had to put Daniel in the lions' den. As he turned away, Darius said he hoped Daniel's God would rescue him. King Darius did not sleep well that night.

As Daniel stood among the lions, he was not afraid, for he knew he had been true to God. Suddenly an angel appeared and shut the lions' mouths so they could not harm Daniel. The angel went away and Daniel slept peacefully among the lions.

The next morning at dawn, King Darius returned. He called to Daniel, asking if his God had saved him. The king was overjoyed when he heard Daniel's voice come up from the den saying he had been saved by an angel. Daniel was taken from the lions' den and the men who had accused him were put in it. Daniel was safe because he had trusted God and remained faithful to Him.

 SS2875

A PROPHET WHO RAN AWAY

"But the Lord provided a great fish to swallow Jonah, and Jonah was inside the fish three days and three nights."

Jonah 1:17

OBJECTS

Craft sticks
Figures of ship, Jonah, and fish (patterns on page 91)
Tape or glue

INTRODUCTION

Before class, reproduce and cut out the figures and attach each to a craft stick.

Begin by telling this story: A boy named Joey got very mad at his mother when she told him to clean up his room. Joey put a shirt, an apple, and his toy car in a paper bag and ran away from home. Joey was not going to listen to his mother anymore, but three blocks from his house Joey changed his mind. It was getting dark and he decided he would rather clean his room and be safe at home! Long ago a prophet did not want to listen to God and he ran away. Listen to what happened to him.

BIBLE STORY

Read or tell in your own words the story on page 44. Hold up the Jonah stick when mentioned. Show the ship with Jonah behind it as if he is on board. When he is thrown from the ship, replace the ship with the fish figure. When Jonah is swallowed by the fish, conceal him behind the fish until he is released.

FOLLOW-UP ACTIVITIES

1. **Coloring Book:** Reproduce for each child the picture and story on page 44. The finished pictures may be filed in individual folders and later compiled into books.

2. **Stick Figure Theater:** You'll need the patterns on page 91, craft sticks, and tape. Reproduce the patterns and give them to the children to color, cut out, and attach to sticks. Let the children use them to act out the story of A Prophet Who Ran Away.

SS2875

A PROPHET WHO RAN AWAY

Jonah 1:1-3:3

Jonah was a prophet of God. God told him to go to the wicked city of Nineveh and preach God's word to them. Jonah did not want to go to some sinful foreign city and preach, so he decided to run away! He went down to Joppa, which was on the sea coast. He found a ship that would take him far away from Nineveh and God—or so Jonah thought.

The ship with Jonah on board sailed out into a calm sea. Then God sent a great wind and storm that was about to break up the ship. The sailors were afraid and called out to their gods to save them. Jonah was below deck, sound asleep. The captain went to him and asked him to call on his God to save them. The sailors thought someone on board had caused this disaster. They decided it must be Jonah. He had told them he was running away from his Lord. They asked him what they could do to make the sea calm again. Jonah said, "Throw me overboard." The sailors did not want to do that! They tried to get control of the ship, but nothing helped. They would all die if they did not do as Jonah said, so they finally threw him into the raging sea. It immediately became calm.

The ship sailed away, leaving Jonah bobbing in the water. As the ship went out of sight, God sent a great fish which swallowed Jonah. For three days and nights Jonah was inside that fish. It was dark and wet and frightening. Jonah did a very good thing—he prayed. On the third day, God told the great fish to spit Jonah up on dry land. For the second time, God told Jonah to go to Nineveh. This time Jonah obeyed the word of the Lord.

 SS2875

A GIFT FROM GOD

"While they were there, the time came for the baby to be born."   Luke 2:6

OBJECTS
Nativity figures—Jesus in a manger, Mary,
   Joseph, and animals
A box
Christmas gift wrap and ribbon

INTRODUCTION
Before class, place the figure of Jesus in a
manger in the box. Wrap with Christmas paper
and ribbon. Print on a small card "A Gift From
God To All The World" and attach it to the
wrapped box.

Show the box to your class and explain that
Christmas is a time to give gifts to people we
love and even to people we don't know. Explain
that this gift is very special because it is from
God to all of them. They will soon learn what is
inside.

BIBLE STORY
Read or tell in your own words the story on
page 46. Place the Mary and Joseph figures on
a table when mentioned. When the animals are
referred to, place them on the table. Before the
last sentence, open the box and reveal God's
gift. Place the figure of Jesus in the manger on
the table.

FOLLOW-UP ACTIVITIES

1. **Coloring Book:** Reproduce for each child the picture and story on page 46. The
   finished pictures may be filed in individual folders and later compiled into books.

2. **A Gift Card:** You'll need Christmas gift wrap, old Christmas cards, small bows,
   paper, and tape.
   Give each child a 6" x 12" piece of wrapping paper and fold it in half. Let him add a
   bow to the outside. Give him a 2" x 2" paper, have him print "A Gift From God" on
   it, and attach it to the card. Have children look through old Christmas cards and
   find pictures of Baby Jesus in His manger. Have them cut out the pictures and glue
   or tape them to the insides of their cards. Encourage them to share their cards with
   people who are alone during the Christmas season or those who are shut-in or ill.

A GIFT FROM GOD
Luke 2:1-7

Long ago a man named Caesar Augustus was a powerful ruler over many lands. He ordered that the people of those lands be counted. Joseph had to go to Bethlehem to be counted.

Joseph lived in Nazareth. He was a carpenter, pledged to marry a young woman named Mary. He was not happy when he heard that he and Mary must travel to Bethlehem. It would be a long, tiring trip for her because she was expecting a very special baby. Joseph knew he had no choice but to go.

They arrived in Bethlehem late at night. The town was bustling with people. Mary was very tired from the long trip and she looked forward to a warm meal and a soft bed, but no rooms were available. An innkeeper with a kind heart said they could sleep in his stable with the animals. At least they would be warm. Mary and Joseph gratefully accepted.

During the night, Mary's child was born. She wrapped Him in soft cloths and placed him on a bed of hay in the animals' manger. In that simple manger lay God's precious gift to all the world, His only Son.

SS2875

THE ANGEL'S GOOD NEWS

"I bring you good news of great joy that will be for all the people."   Luke 2:10b

OBJECTS

Two newspapers
White paper
Nativity picture

INTRODUCTION

Before class print in large letters on white paper: "Good News For All The People." Glue the Nativity picture under the headline. Below the picture, in smaller letters print the words from Luke 2:11–12 and verse 14. Tape the completed paper on the front page of one of the newspapers.

Hold up the other newspaper and ask what is in it (news, weather, sports, etc.). Explain that often the paper has important news to report: man lands on the moon, a war comes to an end, a hurricane is coming, etc. In Bible times God had some super important news to tell the world. It all began on the hills outside the town of Bethlehem.

BIBLE STORY

Read or tell in your own words the story on page 48. Show the second newspaper when the angels bring their message.

FOLLOW-UP ACTIVITIES

1. **Coloring Book:** Reproduce for each child the picture and story on page 48. The finished pictures may be filed in individual folders and later compiled into books.

2. **Make a Newspaper:** You'll need white sheets of paper, markers, and old Christmas cards.
   Help children lay out the front page of a newspaper reporting the events of the first Christmas. Select a name for the paper: Jerusalem Journal, Gospel News, etc. Choose pictures from the cards to illustrate Jesus in a manger, the shepherds, the angels, wise men, etc. Create headlines to match the pictures and have children print short articles under them. Display the completed paper in the church, library, or classroom.

Shining Star Publications, Copyright © 1993   SS2875

THE ANGEL'S GOOD NEWS
Luke 2:8-20

It was nighttime and outside Bethlehem shepherds were watching their flocks to protect them from wild animals. They were settling down for the long night when suddenly a bright light shone all around them and in the midst of it was an angel! The poor men were terrified. Angels did not come to earth every day!

The angel said, "Do not be afraid. I bring you good news of great joy that will be for all the people. Today in the town of David a Savior has been born to you; he is Christ the Lord. This will be a sign to you: You will find a baby wrapped in cloths and lying in a manger."

The shepherds marveled at these words. Their people had been waiting for thousands of years for the Savior. Could it be true? Then to their amazement the angel was joined by many other angels!

These angels praised God and said, "Glory to God in the highest, and on earth peace to men on whom his favor rests."

As soon as the angels returned to heaven, the shepherds discussed what they should do. They agreed to go down to Bethlehem and try to find the baby. They left their sheep and went seeking the Savior.

They found Mary and Joseph and the baby just as the angel had said. They were filled with joy and told the good news to everyone they saw. The grateful shepherds went back to their sheep, glorifying and praising God for all they had heard and seen.

SS2875

A STAR LEADS THE WAY

"When they saw the star, they were overjoyed."   Matthew 2:10

OBJECTS

Apple
Paring knife

INTRODUCTION

Hold up the apple. Explain that God has put something special inside every apple. Ask: Do you know what it is? Using a knife, cut the apple in half around the middle. Open the halves and show the star shape that is made by the seeds. Say: In every apple God has put a star. Long ago a star led some wise men on a long journey. Listen carefully to find out where the star led them and what they found.

BIBLE STORY

Read or tell in your own words the story on page 50. Show the star in the apple when the star is mentioned.

FOLLOW-UP ACTIVITIES

1. **Coloring Book:** Reproduce for each child the picture and story on page 50. The finished pictures may be filed in individual folders and later compiled into books.

2. **Starry snack:** You'll need apples, a knife, yellow construction paper, yarn, and glue.
   Slice apples so that the star shape is in each slice and let them dry out. Give each child a 3" x 3" square of yellow paper on which to glue the slice. Punch a hole in one corner of the paper and attach a loop of yarn so the child may hang the apple star on the Christmas tree. Conclude by passing out apple slices for the children to eat.

SS2875

A STAR LEADS THE WAY
Matthew 2:1-12

King Herod ruled in the land of Judea. He was a cruel and wicked man. One day Magi appeared at his court. These wise and educated men were from a land in the east. The king wondered what had brought them to his country.

The Magi asked, "Where is the one who has been born king of the Jews? We saw his star in the east and have come to worship him."

These words upset King Herod. He was king and no one else. He called his priests and teachers of the Law and asked them where the king of the Jews was to be born. They replied that the Scriptures said it would be Bethlehem.

Herod met with the Magi. He told them, "Go and make a careful search for the child. As soon as you find him, report to me, so that I too may go and worship him."

The Magi did not know how wicked Herod was. They did not realize that he planned to kill the child. They left Jerusalem and began to follow the star once again.

They traveled for many days as the star went ahead of them. Then as they neared the town of Bethlehem, the star stopped. It shone over the house where the child lived. The Magi were overjoyed! The star had led them to the new king!

They entered the house and saw Mary with the child. They bowed down and worshiped him. Then they gave him gifts of gold, incense, and myrrh. These were gifts fit for a king! That night God spoke to the Magi in a dream and warned them not to go back to Herod, but to return to their country another way. They obeyed God's warning.

SS2875

A DOVE FROM HEAVEN

"And a voice from heaven said, 'This is my Son, whom I love; with him I am well pleased.'"

Matthew 3:17

OBJECTS

Dove figurine (or use the pattern on page 93)

INTRODUCTION

Ask your class to tell you the names of some birds. Write the names on a chalkboard or a piece of paper. Ask if any of the birds they have listed are mentioned in the Bible (sparrow, raven, owl, eagle, etc.). If the dove was not suggested, add it at this time. Hold up the dove figurine and say that you are going to tell a story about a heavenly dove.

BIBLE STORY

Read or tell in your own words the story on page 52. When the dove is mentioned show the dove figurine.

FOLLOW-UP ACTIVITIES

1. **Coloring Book:** Reproduce for each child the picture and story on page 52. The finished pictures may be filed in individual folders and later compiled into books.

2. **Dove Search:** You'll need the dove pattern on page 93, paper, and tape.
   Cut out nineteen doves from the pattern. On each dove print one word from the memory verse, Matthew 3:17. Tape the doves around the room. Have the children take turns finding the dove with the word from the verse that you call out. When all nineteen doves have been found, ask children to tape them in the correct order on a wall or bulletin board. Read the completed verse together.

Shining Star Publications, Copyright © 1993 SS2875

A DOVE FROM HEAVEN
Matthew 3:1-17

Jesus' cousin John was a popular preacher. He spoke to people in the Desert of Judea. John wore camel hair clothes and ate locusts and honey. He was a strange man, but people listened to his powerful message about repenting for their sins because the kingdom was near. He baptized many of them in the Jordan River, and it was there that Jesus came to begin His work for God.

John was telling the people, "I baptize with water but one will come after me who is more powerful. I am not fit to even carry His sandals."

Then Jesus came to Jordan and told John He wanted to be baptized. John was amazed. Jesus should baptize him!

Jesus said, "It is proper for us to do this to fulfill all righteousness."

Hearing these words, John agreed. He baptized Jesus Christ, the Son of God, in the Jordan River. As Jesus came up out of the water, heaven opened and the Spirit of God came down in the form of a dove.

The dove came to rest on Jesus and a voice from heaven said, "This is my Son, whom I love; with him I am well pleased."

The dove returned to heaven, then Jesus left the Jordan and went out into the desert.

SS2875

THE FISHERS OF MEN

" 'Come, follow me,' Jesus said, 'and I will make you fishers of men.' "   Matthew 4:19

OBJECTS

A fishing pole made of a stick with attached line
   and a magnet for a hook
Metal paper clips
Paper fish (pattern on page 91)

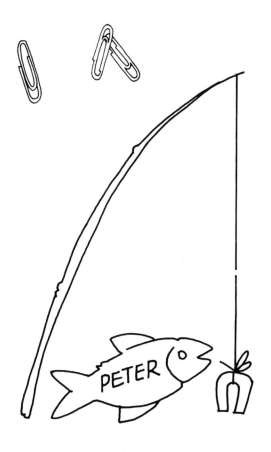

INTRODUCTION

Before class, make the fishing pole. Cut out five fish from the pattern and print the names Peter, Andrew, James, and John on four of them. Slip paper clips on the five fish.

Place a blank fish on the floor. Show children the pole and ask if they have ever been fishing. Call a child forward to "catch" the fish on the floor. Explain that you are going to tell them about four fishermen in the Bible who were called to do some very special fishing.

BIBLE STORY

Read or tell in your own words the story on page 54. Place the four printed fish on the floor. "Catch" each as his name is mentioned.

FOLLOW-UP ACTIVITIES

1. **Coloring Book:** Reproduce for each child the picture and story on page 54. The finished pictures may be filed in individual folders and later compiled into books.

2. **Gone Fishing:** You'll need paper, the fish pattern on page 91, paper clips, and a stick with line and a magnet.

   Using the pattern, cut out twelve fish. Print the name of a disciple on each of them (Matthew 10:2-4). Attach paper clips to the fish. Scatter them on the floor with the names right side up. Give a child the pole and tell her to "catch" the fish that has the name of the disciple described in the clue. Clues: the disciple with the longest name (Bartholomew), the disciple whose name has nine letters in it (Thaddaeus), the one who walked on water (Peter), the brother of Peter (Andrew), the one who betrayed Jesus (Judas Iscariot), the one called the Zealot (Simon), the one who was a doubter (Thomas), the brother of John (James), the tax collector (Matthew), the beloved disciple (John), the son of Alphaeus (James), and the one who told Nathanael about Jesus (Philip). If a child "catches" the wrong fish she must throw it back and give someone else a turn. Continue until all the fish are caught.

THE FISHERS OF MEN

Luke 5:1-11; Matthew 4:18-22

Jesus began His ministry preaching the Word of God. Great crowds came to hear Him speak. At first He had no close followers to help Him. One day He was standing by the Sea of Galilee. People were crowded around Him almost pushing Him into the water! Jesus saw two boats at the water's edge. They had been left there by fishermen who were on the shore, washing their nets. He called to the fishermen and asked if they would take Him out a short way in their boat. Two brothers, Peter and Andrew, agreed to help the preacher.

Jesus sat in the boat and taught the people on the beach. After He finished speaking, Jesus told Peter to go out into the deep water and let down his net to catch fish.

Peter replied, "Master, we have worked hard all night and haven't caught anything, but because you say so, I will let down the nets."

When the brothers began to pull in the nets, they had to call for help from their partners. The net was so full of fish it was about to break. James and John, the sons of Zebedee, came with their boat to help. Soon both boats were so full they began to sink! The fishermen were astonished!

Jesus then said, "Don't be afraid; from now on you will catch men."

Then Andrew, Peter, James, and John pulled their boats up on the shore, left everything they owned, and followed Jesus. They never once regretted that decision.

SS2875

FIVE LOAVES AND TWO FISH

"They all ate and were satisfied."   Mark 6:42

OBJECTS
Five pieces of flat bread (pita)
Two cooked fish cakes
Small basket with a cloth

INTRODUCTION
Before class, place the bread and fish in the basket and cover with the cloth.

Ask: Do you enjoy going on a picnic with family and friends? Doesn't it seem that food eaten outdoors tastes better? Sometimes there are so many people at a picnic, that there isn't enough food to go around. No one likes that to happen. But that is exactly the problem that faced Jesus and His disciples late one afternoon far out in the country.

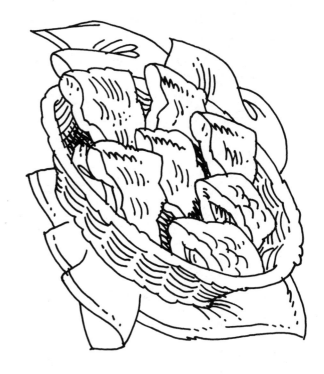

BIBLE STORY
Read or tell in your own words the story on page 56. Take off the cloth and show the five pieces of bread and the two pieces of fish when mentioned.

FOLLOW-UP ACTIVITIES

1. **Coloring Book:** Reproduce for each child the picture and story on page 56. The finished pictures may be filed in individual folders and later compiled into books.

2. **A Simple Lunch:** You'll need pita bread, fish-shaped crackers or cooked fish cakes, drinks, napkins, and cups.

   If weather permits, go outside for lunch. If not, have the children sit on the floor. Give each child a portion of pita bread and fish or crackers on napkins. Serve a cold fruit drink. Be sure to thank God for the meal and for Jesus and His great love. Ask children to pretend they were in the crowd of five thousand. Ask how they would have felt if they had been a part of the miracle of feeding all those people with just five loaves and two fish.

                                              SS2875

FIVE LOAVES AND TWO FISH
Matthew 14:13-21

Jesus had gone to a quiet place to be alone but the crowds followed Him from the towns. He had compassion on them and began to heal the sick.

The hour grew late and the disciples came to Jesus to say that He should send the people away so they could walk to a village and buy food. The crowd numbered over five thousand!

Jesus said, "They do not need to go away. You give them something to eat."

The disciples were stunned. They knew they did not have enough money to feed all those people. When they searched through the great crowd, they could find only five loaves and two fish.

Jesus told them to bring Him the bread and fish. Then He told the people to sit down on the grass. He took the food, and looking up to heaven, gave thanks for it. He began breaking the five loaves into pieces and handing them to the disciples. He told the twelve men to pass the bread out among the people. He did the same for the two fish. The crowd and the disciples kept expecting the food to run out, but Jesus continued breaking off pieces. At last the people had eaten all they could hold and were satisfied. Jesus directed the disciples to pick up the food that was left over. The broken pieces filled twelve baskets! Jesus had fed five thousand people with just five loaves of bread and two small fish.

 SS2875

THE RESCUE

"Immediately Jesus reached out his hand and caught him. 'You of little faith,' he said, 'why did you doubt?' "

Matthew 14:31

OBJECTS

A life preserver or child's inflated swim ring with a short string or rope attached

INTRODUCTION

Show the preserver or ring. Ask your class if they know when it is used. Explain that it is used to rescue people who are about to drown. If a person falls out of a boat or someone gets in trouble while swimming in a pool, the lifeguard can throw the ring for the person to hold on to until he gets to them. Explain that you have a Bible story about a drowning man and how he was rescued.

BIBLE STORY

Read or tell in your own words the story on page 58. When Jesus reaches out to Peter, throw the ring on the floor and begin pulling it back to you.

FOLLOW-UP ACTIVITIES

1. **Coloring Book:** Reproduce for each child the picture and story on page 58. The finished pictures may be filed in individual folders and later compiled into books.

2. **Memory Verse Ring Game:** You'll need a compass, heavy paper, and a plastic drink bottle.

   With a compass, draw on paper a large circle and a smaller circle inside it (large enough to slip over the plastic bottle). Make copies for the children to cut out. Have them print the words of the memory verse, Matthew 14:31, around the ring. Children may then play a game with the rings. Print the name Peter on a strip of paper and attach it to the plastic bottle. Let children throw their rings at the bottle. A "ringer" saves Peter and wins two points. The ring nearest the bottle receives one point.

SS2875

THE RESCUE
Matthew 14:22-33

After Jesus fed the five thousand, He told His disciples to take a boat and sail to the other side of the lake. He said He would join them after He dismissed the huge crowd.

The disciples started across the great lake. Before they had gone very far, a storm came up. The winds were tossing the boat around. The disciples were afraid.

After sending the crowd away, Jesus went up on a mountain to be alone and pray. He knew the disciples were in trouble, so Jesus went down the mountain and to the water's edge. Then He did a wondrous thing. Jesus began walking on top of the water toward the disciples! When they saw Him coming, they were terrified. They thought it was a ghost!

Jesus called to them, "Take courage! It is I. Don't be afraid."

Peter cried, "If it's you, tell me to come to you on the water."

Jesus told Peter to come. Peter got out of the boat and began walking on the water to Jesus. He was doing fine until he took his eyes off Jesus. In that moment he saw the waves and felt the wind, and Peter became afraid. He began to sink and was going to drown! He called to Jesus to save him. Jesus immediately reached out His hand and caught Peter. Jesus took Peter to the boat, and when they climbed in, the storm went away. The amazed disciples declared that Jesus was truly the Son of God.

SS2875

THANK YOU, JESUS

"Then he said to him, 'Rise and go; your faith has made you well.'" Luke 17:19

OBJECTS

Thank-you card (You may make one from the pattern on page 95.)
Small pad of stick-on notes

INTRODUCTION

If you're making a thank-you card, prepare it before class. Print on the inside "Thank you, Jesus." On several stick-on notes print the word leprosy.

Ask children if they are pleased when someone thanks them for helping, giving a present, being well–behaved, etc. Explain that everyone appreciates being thanked for a job well done, but often people don't think to say thank you. Hold up the card but do not open it. Explain that you have a story about ten men who should have said thank you. Encourage children to listen carefully to learn how many did.

BIBLE STORY

Read or tell in your own words the story on page 60. Place stick-on notes on your arms and legs when the lepers appear in the story. Remove them when they are healed. When one leper returns to say thank you, show the card and open it up to reveal the message.

FOLLOW-UP ACTIVITIES

1. **Coloring Book:** Reproduce for each child the picture and story on page 60. The finished pictures may be filed in individual folders and later compiled into books.

2. **Thank-You Notes:** You'll need paper, crayons or markers, scissors, and the pattern on page 95.
   Reproduce the thank-you note pattern for each child to color, cut out, and fold to form a card. Each child should think of someone she wants to thank, then print a message to that person on the inside of the card.

THANK YOU, JESUS
Luke 17:11-19

Jesus was on His way to Jerusalem, traveling near the border between Samaria and Galilee. He was going into a village when He met ten men standing alongside the road. The men were not allowed in the village because they had leprosy. Their bodies were covered with terrible sores.

The lepers called out to Jesus, "Jesus, Master, have pity on us!"

They knew who Jesus was. They must have heard of His healing miracles. Jesus told the men to show themselves to the priests. The priests had the power to say if a person was fit to come in contact with others. The lepers did not hesitate; they started down the road. As they ran along, the ten men realized that the terrible sores were disappearing from their bodies. They were overjoyed!

One of them, a Samaritan, came running back to Jesus. He was praising God with a loud voice. He threw himself at Jesus' feet and thanked Him.

Jesus looked around and said, "Were not ten cleansed? Where are the other nine?"

Those nine men could be seen far down the road, hurrying to the priests. Only one man had come back to thank Jesus, and he was a Samaritan. They were people hated by most Jews.

Jesus was pleased with the Samaritan. He said, "Rise and go; your faith has made you well."

SS2875

MIRACLE MUD

"Therefore the Pharisees also asked him how he had received his sight. 'He put mud on my eyes,' the man replied, 'and I washed, and now I see.'" John 9:15

OBJECTS

Container of dirt
Container of water
Spoon

INTRODUCTION

Ask the children: Have you ever made mud pies? Did you have a good time? Mud can be fun, but it can also be a mess, especially when it is tracked into the house on muddy shoes or gets on clean clothes. In the Bible there is a story of a man making mud. Listen to see if the mud was good or bad.

BIBLE STORY

Read or tell in your own words the story on page 62. As you talk about Jesus making mud, pour water into a container of dirt and stir with a spoon to make thick mud.

FOLLOW-UP ACTIVITIES

1. **Coloring Book:** Reproduce for each child the picture and story on page 62. The finished pictures may be filed in individual folders and later compiled into books.

2. **"Mud" Fun:** Make clay with the following recipe or purchase modeling clay.
Clay may be made with 1 cup salt, ½ cup cornstarch, ½ cup boiling water, and food coloring. Stir all ingredients together over low heat until smooth. Store in sealed containers. Give children portions of clay and have them make animals or people or whatever they choose. Remind them that Jesus used a bit of mud to make one man very happy. Suggest that they share what they make.

MIRACLE MUD
John 9

One day Jesus was walking near the Pool of Siloam. Sitting by the water was a man who had been blind from birth. He had never seen a cloud or a tree or a human face. Because of his blindness he was unable to work and had to beg. The disciples, who were with Jesus, asked what the man or his parents had done for him to be punished in such a way.

Jesus replied, "Neither this man nor his parents sinned, but this happened so that the work of God might be displayed in his life."

Having said that, Jesus reached down and scooped up some dirt from the road. He spat into it, then stirred the dirt and saliva to make mud. He put some mud on the blind man's eyes. Jesus told the man to go to the Pool of Siloam and wash the mud from his eyes. The man did as Jesus said. As the water cleared the mud off his eyes, he began to blink. Could it be that he saw a little light? Wait! There was more! He saw a white cloud floating in a blue sky and all around the pool there were green trees. Then he turned and looked on the first face he had ever seen, the kind face of Jesus!

The man went around telling everyone that he could see. Some did not believe that he was the once-blind beggar. The Pharisees hated Jesus and tried to use the man to cause trouble for Him. At first the healed man thought Jesus was a prophet, but in time he came to know who Jesus truly was–the only Son of God!

SS2875

THE LOST SHEEP

"Then he calls his friends and neighbors together and says, 'Rejoice with me; I have found my lost sheep.'"

Luke 15:6b

OBJECTS
Piece of wool material or a wool sweater
Picture of sheep or a sheep figure made from the pattern on page 93

INTRODUCTION
Make the sheep figure before class and hide the figure or picture in the room before the children arrive.

Ask your class why people raise sheep. Explain that they are raised for food and for their wool. The wool can be spun and made into thread to make cloth. (Show the material or sweater.) In Bible times, shepherds raised sheep for these same reasons. Every sheep was important to the shepherd because it meant food on the table and money for his family. Jesus once told a story of a shepherd who lost one sheep. Encourage the children to listen to see if he found it.

BIBLE STORY
Read or tell in your own words the story on page 64. When the shepherd begins looking for his lost sheep, get up and move around the room as if searching for it. "Find" the sheep picture or figure at the appropriate time.

FOLLOW-UP ACTIVITIES
1. **Coloring Book:** Reproduce for each child the picture and story on page 64. The finished pictures may be filed in individual folders and later compiled into books.

2. **Finding the Lost Sheep:** You'll need the sheep pattern on page 93, paper, cotton balls, and white glue.
   Reproduce the sheep pattern for each child to cut out and cover with cotton balls. The cotton may be pulled apart and dipped into white glue. When the sheep are dry, children may take turns hiding them and having others search for them.

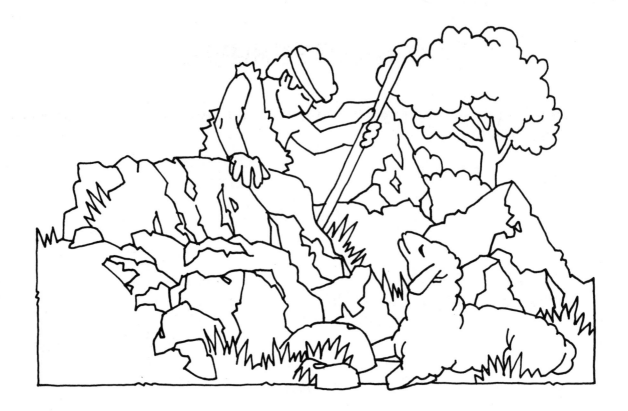

THE LOST SHEEP

Luke 15:3-7

Jesus often taught with a parable—a story with a lesson. This is one about a shepherd and his sheep.

The shepherd was very proud of his flock. He had exactly 100 sheep. They were going to bring a good price at the market. Each day he took them out to the pasture to let them eat their fill. They were getting very fat! At night he brought them back to their pen. As they walked through the narrow opening, he counted to make sure all 100 were there.

One day, almost at dark, he was carefully counting as the sheep passed through. He said, "96, 97, 98, 99."

The shepherd stopped. Where was sheep number 100? He looked all around the outside of the pen, but no sheep. It was getting very late. The shepherd had worked all day and he was hungry. He could have forgotten the lost sheep and left it to the wolves, who would surely catch and eat it. But he didn't. The shepherd drew his cloak around him and, taking his long, curved staff, went out searching for his one lost sheep.

He had to look for a long time, but he finally found the sheep caught in a bramble bush. He gently released it from the thorns, wrapped it in his cloak, and carried the sheep home. On the way he stopped at his neighbors' house and told them his good news. They all rejoiced with the shepherd because he had found his lost sheep.

Jesus said that, in the same way, there would be more rejoicing in heaven over one sinner who repents than over 99 righteous persons who do not need to repent.

Shining Star Publications, Copyright © 1993 SS2875

TWO HOUSEBUILDERS

"Therefore everyone who hears these words of mine and puts them into practice is like a wise man who built his house on the rock."

Matthew 7:24

OBJECTS

A large rock or brick
A container of sand or soft dirt
Two house figures (pattern on page 95)

INTRODUCTION

Before class, make two houses from the pattern. Cut on the line, then fold half to the back and half to the front. Tape one house to a rock and set the other in sand.

Ask children: What is your house made of? Explain that people build their homes to be as strong as possible. Jesus once told a story of some housebuilders. Children should listen to see if the builders were good at their jobs.

BIBLE STORY

Read or tell in your own words the story on page 66. Place the two houses in front of the children. When the house on the rock is mentioned, shake the rock and show that the house stands. When the house on the sand is mentioned, shake the container of sand and cause that house to fall over.

FOLLOW-UP ACTIVITIES

1. **Coloring Book:** Reproduce for each child the picture and story on page 66. The finished pictures may be filed in individual folders and later compiled into books.

2. **Paperweight:** You'll need large rocks, the house pattern on page 95, and tape. Reproduce the house pattern for each child to color, cut out, and fold the stand-up tabs on the bottom. Give each child a rock on which to tape the house. Help the child print on a strip of paper "I Build On The Solid Rock," and tape it to the rock.

TWO HOUSEBUILDERS
Matthew 7:24-29

Jesus wanted people to understand that they must listen to His words and also put them into practice. He told them a parable about two housebuilders.

The men were very good builders. They knew how to mix straw and clay together to make bricks for their houses. They knew how to make a roof so rain could not get in. Their houses would be the best in all the village.

First they had to decide where to build. The first man looked all around the town. He carried a shovel and dug holes here and there. The other man thought this was foolishness. He went off to do his own searching.

The first builder dug a hole three feet deep and declared that this was the place for his house. At the bottom of the hole the man had hit solid rock. He knew that any house built here would never fall because it would be built on a firm foundation.

The second builder looked all around and decided to build his house near the seashore. It would be cooler there and everyone would be better able to see his new home. He began building on the soft sand and gave no thought to the foundation.

The men completed their houses and moved their families into them. Not long after, a terrible storm blew in from the sea. The wind and rain beat against the houses. The man who had built on the solid rock was not worried. The man who had built on the sand soon regretted it. The storm shook his house and it fell with a great crash.

If people practice what Jesus teaches, they are building their lives on solid rock!

 SS2875

THE SEED PLANTER

"Others, like seed sown on good soil, hear the word, accept it, and produce a crop—thirty, sixty or even a hundred times what was sown."   Mark 4:20

OBJECTS
Container of clay and container of rocks
Container of weeds and container of soil
Large seeds and craft sticks
Bible
Plant patterns on page 94

INTRODUCTION
Before class reproduce and cut out the four plants from the patterns. Attach them to craft sticks.

Place a packet of seeds inside your Bible. Show the Bible. Say: Inside this book are seeds which, if planted in the right way, can help you grow into the person God wants you to be. (Open the Bible and show the seeds.) Every time you learn something from the Bible, it is like a seed growing inside you. Jesus once told a story about a farmer who planted seeds. He said the seed was the Word of God. Listen to find out what happened to those seeds.

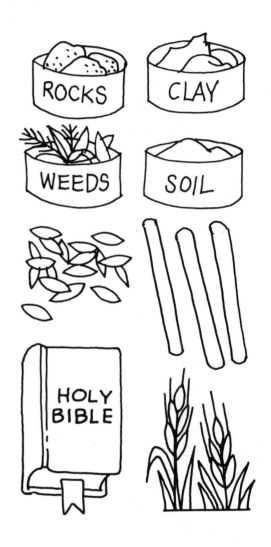

BIBLE STORY
Read or tell in your own words the story on page 68. With the containers in front of you, place a seed and then the plant in the correct container as it is mentioned.

FOLLOW-UP ACTIVITIES
1. **Coloring Book:** Reproduce for each child the picture and story on page 68. The finished pictures may be filed in individual folders and later compiled into books.

2. **Egg Carton Seed Planters:** You'll need egg cartons, the plant patterns on page 94, soil, and craft sticks.
   Cut egg cartons into four cup sections and give a section to each child to fill with soil. Reproduce the four plant patterns for each child to color, cut out, tape to sticks, and place in the soil. Ask which plant would please Jesus.

THE SEED PLANTER
Mark 4:2-20

Jesus once told a parable about a farmer who went out to plant seed.

The farmer carried his seeds in a large bag. He took handfuls of seeds from the bag and threw them out on the ground as he walked along. His first handful of seed landed on a nearby road. It was hard dirt, beaten down by passing carts. The seed just sat on top of the ground and birds came and ate it. The next handful fell in a rocky place in the field. Those plants grew up quickly, but the soil was not good enough for them to put down roots. On the first hot day, the plants withered and died. The third handful of seeds fell in a patch of weeds full of thorns. The plants came up, but the weeds were stronger and soon choked the farmer's plants until they died. The fourth handful of seeds landed on good soil. There they sprouted and began to grow. Those plants lived and produced a huge crop for the farmer.

Jesus said the seeds were like the Word of God. Some people hear the Word but they are like the hard ground. They refuse to believe. Some people hear the Word and rejoice in it, but, like the seed in the rocky place, they don't let it take root in their hearts. Some people hear the Word, but they let the worries of life and the desire for money overcome them. Like the seeds among the weeds, the Word is choked out and bears no fruit. Some people are like the good soil. They hear the Word and try every day to live by it. Each day they produce blessings for themselves and for others.

Shining Star Publications, Copyright © 1993

SS2875

A KIND MAN

"The expert in the law replied, 'The one who had mercy on him.' Jesus told him, 'Go and do likewise.'"

Luke 10:37

OBJECTS

Adhesive bandage
Ointment

INTRODUCTION

Tell this story: A young girl who was roller skating fell and cut her arm. She began to cry, and her mother came running to find out what had happened. The girl took off her skates and they went inside. Her mother washed the cut and put on some ointment and a bandage. (Show the ointment and bandage.) She gave her daughter a big hug. The little girl stopped crying. She felt better. What do you think made the girl feel better: the ointment, the bandage, or her mother's gentle caring and big hug? Jesus once told a story about a kind man who made a man he met on the road feel much better.

BIBLE STORY

Read or tell in your own words the story on page 70. Ask a child to help you. When the Samaritan cares for the man's wounds, put ointment and a bandage on the child's hand.

FOLLOW-UP ACTIVITIES

1. **Coloring Book:** Reproduce for each child the picture and story on page 70. The finished pictures may be filed in individual folders and later compiled into books.

2. **Get Well Card:** You'll need adhesive bandages and sheets of paper.
   Fold sheets of paper into fourths like greeting cards. Give each child a card and a bandage. Have them print "Sorry You Are Sick" on the outside of the card and place the bandage next to the words. On the inside they may print "Hope You Get Well Soon." Encourage children to give their cards to sick friends.

A KIND MAN
Luke 10:25-37

An expert in the law was questioning Jesus. When Jesus said we should love our neighbors, the lawyer asked, "Who is my neighbor?" Jesus answered by telling this story:

A man was going to Jericho when he was attacked by robbers. They beat him and took his clothes, leaving him half dead.

A priest came by on the road. He saw the man, but did not want to get involved, so he passed by on the other side of the road. Next a Levite rode by and saw the injured man, but he also passed by on the other side.

A Samaritan was also traveling on the road. Samaritans were not liked by Jews. When the Samaritan saw the man, he went straight to him! When he saw how badly hurt the man was, the Samaritan took pity on him. He put oil and wine on the man's wounds and bandaged them. He put the injured man on his donkey and took him to an inn. He cared for him through the night and the next day he gave the innkeeper two silver coins and told him to look after the man. The Samaritan said if the innkeeper needed more, he would pay it when he returned.

Jesus asked the expert in the law which of the three men was a neighbor to the man who fell into the hands of robbers. The expert replied that it was the one who showed mercy.

Jesus told him, "Go and do likewise."

SS2875

SHE GAVE ALL SHE HAD

"But she out of her poverty put in all she had to live on."   Luke 21:4b

OBJECTS
Two pennies wrapped in cloth
Small basket
Bag of coins

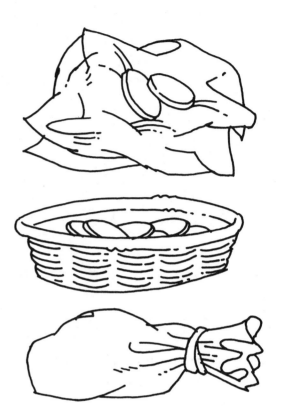

INTRODUCTION
Write the word "offering" on the chalkboard or a piece of paper. Ask your class: What does this word mean? How is the offering taken in our church? Explain that in Bible times people brought their offerings to the great temple. They placed their money into the offering chest, often while people watched. It is there that our story begins.

BIBLE STORY
Read or tell in your own words the story on page 72. When the rich man puts in his coins, pour the coins from the bag into the basket. When the widow puts in her offering, remove the pennies from the cloth and place them in the basket.

FOLLOW-UP ACTIVITIES

1. **Coloring Book:** Reproduce for each child the picture and story on page 72. The finished pictures may be filed in individual folders and later compiled into books.

2. **Giving an Offering:** You'll need pint-size milk cartons, pennies, tape, and stickers or seals.
   Provide a rinsed-out milk carton for each child. (Ask your school cafeteria to save empties for you.) Tape the opening closed and cut a slit in the top. Have children cover the outside of their cartons with a variety of religious or nature stickers and seals. Give children two pennies each to begin an offering. Suggest that they find chores to do and, when they are paid, put all or a portion of the money in their cartons. The class may decide together which Sunday they will take their offerings to church and give them to God.

SHE GAVE ALL SHE HAD
Luke 21:1-4

During the final week of Jesus' ministry on earth, He often went to the temple to speak to people. One day when He had finished speaking, He looked up and saw people putting their gifts into the temple treasury.

A rich man was next in line. He enjoyed showing off his great wealth. He opened the bag holding his offering and held it up so that the coins poured into the treasury box with a loud noise. Many people turned around and watched. They whispered about such a rich gift. God would surely be pleased.

The next person was a woman. She was a very poor widow. She approached the treasury box with her head down. She appeared to be praying. Then the woman opened a small cloth in her hand and drew out two copper coins. She gently placed them in the box and turned to leave.

Jesus said, "I tell you the truth, this poor widow has put in more than all the others. All these people gave their gifts out of their wealth; but she out of her poverty put in all she had to live on."

In that moment the poor widow was the richest woman in the world!

SS2875

THE LAST SUPPER

"And he said to them, 'I have eagerly desired to eat this Passover with you before I suffer.'"

Luke 22:15

OBJECTS

Goblet or cup filled with grape juice
Flat bread (pita)
Passover meal food (patterns on page 96)

INTRODUCTION

Before class reproduce and cut out the food patterns and glue them on paper.

Say: I want to tell you about a special meal. It was first served in the time of Moses when the angel of death was passing over the houses of those who believed in God. This meal was called the Passover. (Point to each food as mentioned.) The people ate roasted lamb to remind them that God provided for them. They ate bitter herbs with sauce to remind them of their suffering in Egypt. They ate unleavened bread to remind them that they were going to leave Egypt in great haste. They also drank wine with their Passover meal. After that, the Passover was celebrated each year by faithful Jews. This was the meal that Jesus ate with His disciples. It was to be His last supper.

BIBLE STORY

Read or tell in your own words the story on page 74. Show the bread and cup of juice when mentioned.

FOLLOW-UP ACTIVITIES

1. **Coloring Book:** Reproduce for each child the picture and story on page 74. The finished pictures may be filed in individual folders and later compiled into books.

2. **A Special Meal:** You'll need the food patterns on page 96, paper place mats or sheets of paper, and glue.
   Reproduce the patterns for each child to color and cut out. Provide a place mat or sheet of paper on which to glue the food to look like a table for the Passover meal.

THE LAST SUPPER
Luke 22:7-22

In Jerusalem it was time to celebrate the Passover. Jesus knew He would soon die and He wanted to have a last meal with His disciples. He sent for Peter and John. He told them to go and make preparations for the Passover. They asked where they should prepare the meal since they had no house of their own.

Jesus answered, "Go into the city and you will meet a man carrying a jar of water. Follow him into the house he enters. Then say to the owner that I ask where the guest room is that I may eat the Passover. He will show you an upper room. Make preparations there."

It happened as Jesus had said, and Peter and John prepared the meal. Jesus and the disciples sat at the table and began the celebration. Certain things were to be done and said at the Passover–it was traditional. Jesus changed that when He took the bread, broke it, and passed it to the disciples, saying that this was His body given for them. Then Jesus took the cup of wine and passed it around to the disciples, saying that this was His blood which was poured out for them. The disciples did not really understand what Jesus meant. Later that night, Jesus was arrested. The next day His body was broken and His blood shed on the cruel cross. Only then did the disciples understand.

Today in churches all over the world this special meal is remembered–not as the Passover–but as the Last Supper.

SS2875

JESUS LIVES!

"He is not here; he has risen, just as he said. Come and see the place where he lay."

Matthew 28:6

OBJECTS
A live tulip plant or tulips made from the instructions under follow-up activities

INTRODUCTION
Tell the following story: On Easter morning a boy was on his hands and knees peering down at the ground. His father asked what he was doing. The boy said he was looking for spring. The father asked if he had found it. The boy replied, "Yes sir! The tulips Mom planted are coming up." Sure enough, little green sprouts were all along the front fence. The tulip bulbs had been under the dark, cold ground all winter, waiting until spring to push up through the earth. Soon the plants would grow tall and there would be red, yellow, pink, purple, orange, and violet tulips. (Show tulips.) At church, the boy and his father heard how God's Son had been in a cold, dark tomb. Then a glorious miracle caused God's love to bloom all over the world.

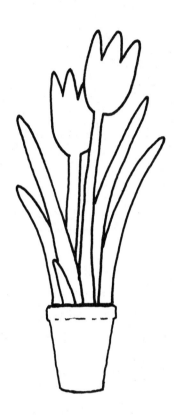

BIBLE STORY
Read or tell in your own words the story on page 76. Place the tulips beside you.

FOLLOW-UP ACTIVITIES
1. **Coloring Book:** Reproduce for each child the picture and story on page 76. The finished pictures may be filed in individual folders and later compiled into books.

2. **Tulip Time:** You'll need Styrofoam™ egg cartons, green pipe cleaners, the leaf patterns on page 95, construction paper, and Styrofoam™ cups.
   Cut the cartons into individual cups. Reproduce the leaf patterns for each tulip and cut them out of green paper. Have children push pipe cleaners through the bottoms of the egg cups, then push the leaves up the "stems" until they touch the egg cups. Make handles for Styrofoam™ cups with pipe cleaners. Place the tulips in the cups. Children may like to give them as Easter gifts.

Shining Star Publications, Copyright © 1993
SS2875

JESUS LIVES!
Matthew 27:58-60; 28:1-8

On Friday Jesus was nailed to the cross and there He died. His followers were over-whelmed with grief. Joseph of Arimathea came and took down the body. He carried it to a garden where his own tomb was located and placed the body inside. He rolled a great stone in front of the entrance and went away to grieve.

Jesus' body lay in that cold, dark tomb all of Friday night. It lay there all through Saturday and into the night. On the third day, as the sun rose, some of the women who followed Jesus came into the garden. They planned to prepare the body with spices. There had not been time on Friday, and they were not allowed to do it on Saturday, the Jewish Sabbath. As they neared the tomb, they saw that the great stone in front of the tomb had been rolled aside and, wonder of wonders, sitting on the stone was an angel! His clothes were snow white and he shone like bright lightning.

The angel said to the women, "Do not be afraid, for I know you are looking for Jesus, who was crucified. He is not here; he has risen, just as he said. Come and see the place where he lay."

The women peered into the tomb. It was no longer a cold and dark place. As the morning sunlight streamed into it, the women saw that it was empty! Jesus had risen from the dead! The women hurried to Jerusalem to spread the good news that Jesus lives!

Shining Star Publications, Copyright © 1993 SS2875

THE ROAD TO DAMASCUS

" 'Who are you, Lord?' Saul asked. 'I am Jesus, whom you are persecuting,' he replied."

Acts 9:5

OBJECTS
A strip of cloth to use as a blindfold

INTRODUCTION
Ask a child to come forward. Tie the cloth over his eyes. Have the other children move around to different seats. Then tell the blindfolded child to touch the face of one of the children and see if he knows who it is. If he guesses incorrectly, tell the other child to say something to identify herself: color of hair, clothes, etc. When the child has guessed correctly, remove the blindfold and say: There was a man in the Bible who was blind to the love of Jesus until something wonderful happened to him on the road to Damascus.

BIBLE STORY
Read or tell in your own words the story on page 78. Tie the cloth over your eyes when Saul becomes blind and remove it when he is healed.

FOLLOW-UP ACTIVITIES

1. **Coloring Book:** Reproduce for each child the picture and story on page 78. The finished pictures may be filed in individual folders and later compiled into books.

2. **Seeking Saul:** You'll need a strip of paper and a piece of cloth.
   Print on the strip of paper "Saul." Choose one child to be the seeker. Tie the cloth over that child's eyes. Pin or tape the strip of paper on a second child. Have the class stand in a large circle with the blindfolded child in the center. Tell that child to try to touch the one who is Saul. If he does, he can take off the blindfold and choose someone else to be in the center. Any child who is touched but is not Saul, must sit down outside the circle. When Saul is found, everyone can get back in the circle and start the game over with a new seeker and a new Saul.

Shining Star Publications, Copyright © 1993 SS2875

THE ROAD TO DAMASCUS

Acts 9:1-22

Jesus had returned to heaven and His followers were preaching and sharing His message. A man named Saul who did not believe in Jesus was persecuting His followers. He was going to Damascus to arrest any believers that he found there.

Not far from Damascus a light suddenly flashed from heaven and shone all around Saul. He had to close his eyes to shield them from the brightness and he fell to the ground. Then Saul heard a voice saying, "Saul, Saul, why do you persecute me?"

Saul asked who was speaking. The voice answered, "I am Jesus, whom you are persecuting. Now get up and go into the city, and you will be told what you must do."

The men traveling with Saul heard the sound but they did not see anything. They helped Saul up. When he opened his eyes, he could not see and the men had to lead him into Damascus.

Three days later Saul still could not see. In the meantime, the Lord spoke to a believer named Ananias. He told Ananias, "Go to a man named Saul who is praying. He has seen you in a vision in which you healed his blindness."

Ananias, knowing the name of Saul, was frightened and did not want to go. The Lord said He had chosen Saul for a special mission. Ananias obeyed and went. He told Saul he had been sent by the One who had appeared to him on the road to Damascus. Ananias put his hands on Saul and immediately he could see again. Saul was baptized, then went to the synagogue in Damascus and began preaching about Jesus. All who heard him were astonished!

SS2875

A KIND WOMAN

"In Joppa there was a disciple named Tabitha (which, when translated, is Dorcas), who was always doing good and helping the poor."   Acts 9:36

OBJECTS
A spool of thread and a needle
A container of straight pins

INTRODUCTION
Show the spool of thread and the needle. Explain that these are used to make or mend clothes. Show the container of straight pins. Explain that people who sew use straight pins to hold the material together. One company that made straight pins was called the Dorcas Company. They chose that name for a very special reason. Encourage children to listen as you tell the story to discover why they decided to become the Dorcas Company.

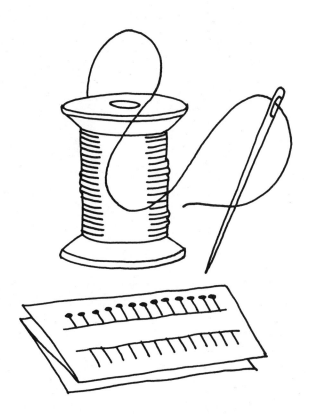

BIBLE STORY
Read or tell in your own words the story on page 80. Show the needle, thread, and pins when Dorcas and her work are mentioned. Ask at the end of the story why the company was named Dorcas.

FOLLOW-UP ACTIVITIES

1. **Coloring Book:** Reproduce for each child the picture and story on page 80. The finished pictures may be filed in individual folders and later compiled into books.

2. **Mobile:** You'll need the robe pattern on page 88, yarn, a hole punch, blunt needles, and cardboard.
   Reproduce the robe pattern for each child to glue to a piece of lightweight cardboard. Using a hole punch, make holes 1/2" apart around the outline of the robe. Provide a length of yarn with a knot for each child. Let her "sew" around the robe. Older children may use needles. Younger children may thread the yarn in and out through the holes.

A KIND WOMAN

Acts 9:36-42

Jesus' disciples went around preaching and healing and doing good works. The apostle Peter had traveled to Lydda to visit the believers there when two men from nearby Joppa came looking for him.

They said to Peter, "Please come at once!"

The men explained that a follower of Jesus named Dorcas had suddenly died. She was well loved by the people of Joppa, and they had come to get Peter to help. They believed Peter could perform a miracle and bring Dorcas back to life.

Peter agreed to go with the men. He probably wondered about this woman who was so loved by her friends and neighbors. When he arrived at Dorcas' house, he was taken to an upstairs room. Many women stood around the dead body, crying. They pleaded with Peter to help. They showed him the robes and other clothing Dorcas had sewn for them. They told of all the other good things the kind woman had done. Peter now understood why Dorcas was so loved.

Peter sent them all out of the room, then he got down on his knees and prayed. He turned to the body of the dead woman and told her to get up. In a split second Dorcas' eyes opened and she sat up! Peter helped her to her feet, then he called the women and presented Dorcas to them alive and well!

Word of this great miracle spread all through Joppa, and many people believed in the Lord because of it.

 SS2875

A PRISON ESCAPE

"Now I know without a doubt that the Lord sent his angel and rescued me from Herod's clutches. . . ."

Acts 12:11

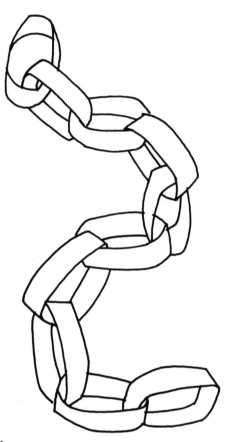

OBJECTS

A paper chain made from strips of paper and tape

INTRODUCTION

Before class, make a long chain with the paper strips and tape.

Show the paper chain and say: If this were made of strong metal, it could not be easily broken. How would you break a metal chain? Explain that a man in the Bible was chained to two soldiers. He could not break the chains to escape, but God could!

BIBLE STORY

Read or tell in your own words the story on page 82. Slip the paper chain over your wrists when Peter is imprisoned. Break it at the appropriate time in the story.

FOLLOW-UP ACTIVITIES

1. **Coloring Book:** Reproduce for each child the picture and story on page 82. The finished pictures may be filed in individual folders and later compiled into books.

2. **Mobile:** You'll need paper chains, six larger strips of paper, and tape.
   Make two paper chains. On the larger strips of paper print "Herod, Peter, guard, guard, angel, and Rhoda." Choose six children to act out these roles. Tape a strip on each. Use the paper chains to bind Peter to the guards. The remainder of the class may be soldiers in the prison or followers at the house. Using the Bible story as a guide, assist children in writing a script with dialogue for Herod, Peter, angel, and Rhoda, or they may pantomime the Bible story as it is written. Ask one child to be a narrator and read the story of A Prison Escape as the others act out their assigned roles.

A PRISON ESCAPE

Acts 12:1-18

Peter was preaching about Jesus. King Herod ordered him arrested. He said, "Put him in prison with chains and guard him well. I will put him on trial after Passover."

While Peter was in prison, Jesus' followers prayed for his safe return. On the night before his trial, Peter slept between two of the guards. He was bound to them with chains and other guards stood at the prison entrance. Suddenly an angel appeared in the cell. He struck Peter and said, "Quick, get up!" The chains fell from Peter's wrists but the guards did not wake up. The angel told Peter to put on his clothes and sandals and follow him. Peter did as he was told, but he wasn't sure if it was real or a dream. He and the angel passed the two guards and the iron gate opened all by itself! They walked through it down a long street, then the angel left Peter.

Peter exclaimed, "Now I know without a doubt that the Lord has rescued me."

He hurried to the house of Mary, mother of John, where the believers had gathered to pray for him. He knocked on the door. A servant girl named Rhoda asked, "Who is there?" Peter identified himself. When Rhoda recognized his voice, she went to tell the others, leaving Peter standing at the door!

Rhoda exclaimed, "Peter is at the door!" The others thought she was out of her mind. They finally went to open the door and were astonished to see Peter standing there. He told them about his wonderful prison escape.

                    SS2875

A JAILER FINDS THE KEY

"He then brought them out and asked, 'Sirs, what must I do to be saved?' They replied, 'Believe in the Lord Jesus, and you will be saved.' "   Acts 16:30–31a

OBJECTS
Assorted keys of all sizes on a ring

INTRODUCTION
Before class trace around one large key, print "Jesus" on it, and cut it out.

Show the keys and ask: What are keys used for? What kind of things do you put a lock on? Explain that a jail or prison has a lock. The keys are kept by the jailer, and only he can open the door. Children should listen carefully to learn what happened to a jailer in the Bible who discovered a new kind of key.

BIBLE STORY
Read or tell in your own words the story on page 84. Jangle the keys whenever the jailer is mentioned. Show the cutout key with Jesus printed on it at the end of the story.

FOLLOW-UP ACTIVITIES

1. **Coloring Book:** Reproduce for each child the picture and story on page 84. The finished pictures may be filed in individual folders and later compiled into books.

2. **A Key Verse:** You'll need keys, paper, and pencils.
   Trace ten keys on paper. Print on them these ten words: "Believe In The Lord Jesus, And You Will Be Saved." Reproduce a sheet for each child. Tell children that these ten keys hold words that are the most important in the entire Bible. Have each child cut out the keys and glue them in correct order on a sheet of paper. The pastor may be invited to share with the class as they put together the Key Verse. Then he may guide the discussion of the children's own personal beliefs about Jesus. Pray that this time may be used by God in a special way.

A JAILER FINDS THE KEY

Acts 16:16-34

Paul, who was once called Saul, and Silas had cast an evil spirit out of a young girl. An angry crowd beat Paul and Silas and had them put in prison. A jailer was told to guard them. He put them deep in the prison and placed their feet in stocks. About midnight, Paul and Silas were praying and singing hymns. The other prisoners listened to them. Suddenly there was an earthquake! The prison doors all flew open and everyone's chains came loose. Paul and Silas were even freed from the stocks. The jailer awoke and when he saw that the doors were open, he drew his sword to kill himself. He knew he would die when the leaders found out he had let all the prisoners escape.

But Paul shouted, "Don't harm yourself! We are all here!"

The jailer called for a light and rushed in to Paul and Silas. He took them out of the cell and asked, "Sirs, what must I do to be saved?"

They replied, "Believe in the Lord Jesus, and you will be saved—you and your household."

The jailer took Paul and Silas to his house. He washed their wounds, and he and his family listened as they were told about Jesus. That night the jailer and his whole household were baptized. He had a great meal set before Paul and Silas. The jailer wanted to celebrate because he was filled with joy that he and his whole family had come to believe in God!

SS2875

"GOD MADE IT ALL" PATTERNS

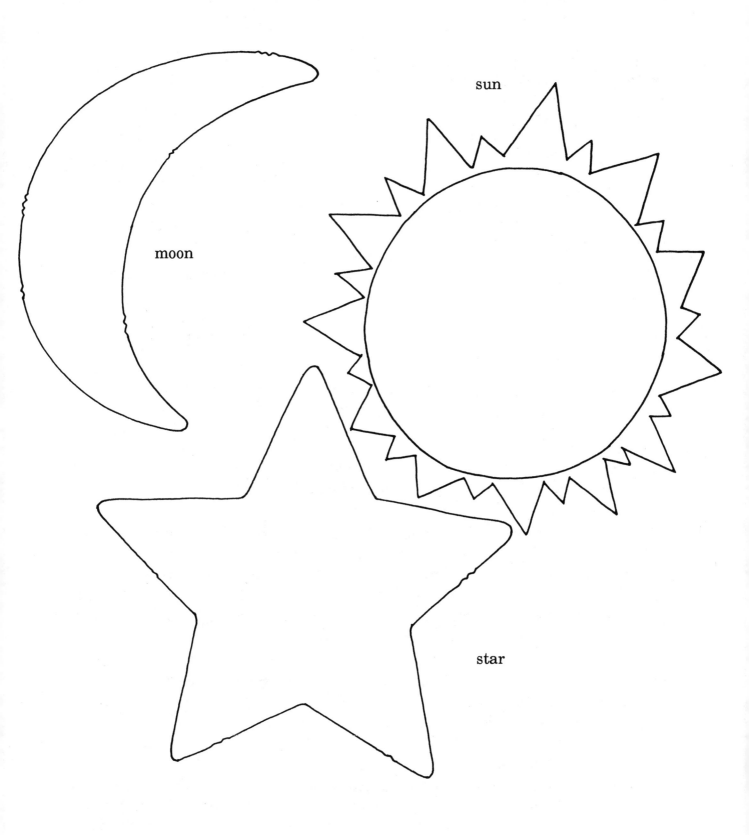

moon

sun

star

SS2875

"A SIGN IN THE SKY" PATTERNS

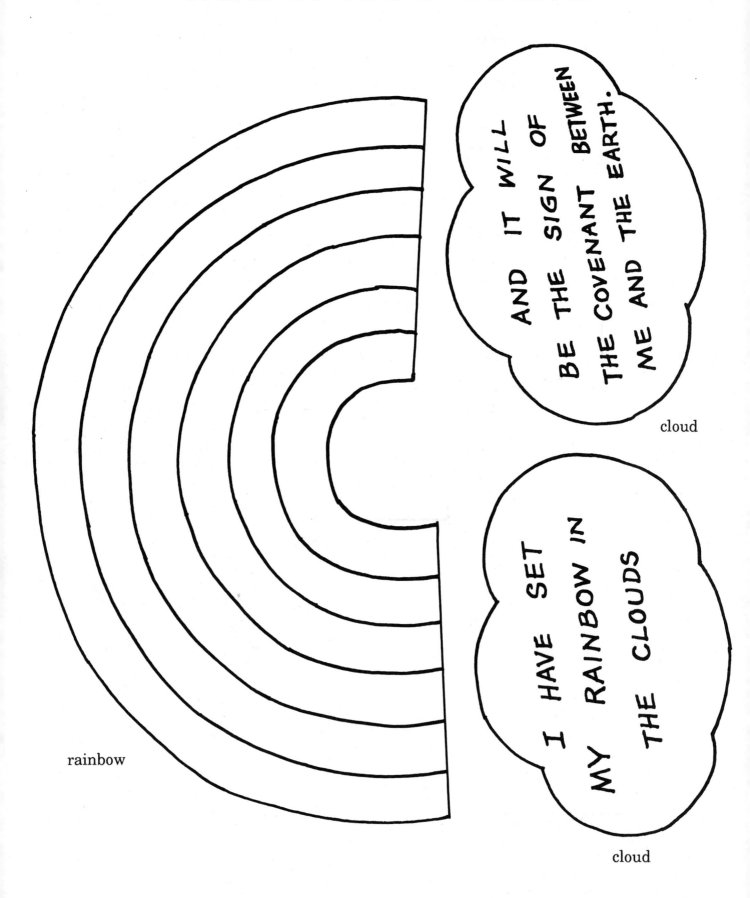

rainbow

cloud

cloud

SS2875

"JACOB'S DREAM" PATTERNS

angel ascending

stairway

angel descending

SS2875

"A SPECIAL ROBE" PATTERNS

Joseph

robe

"A SHEPHERD BECOMES KING" PATTERNS

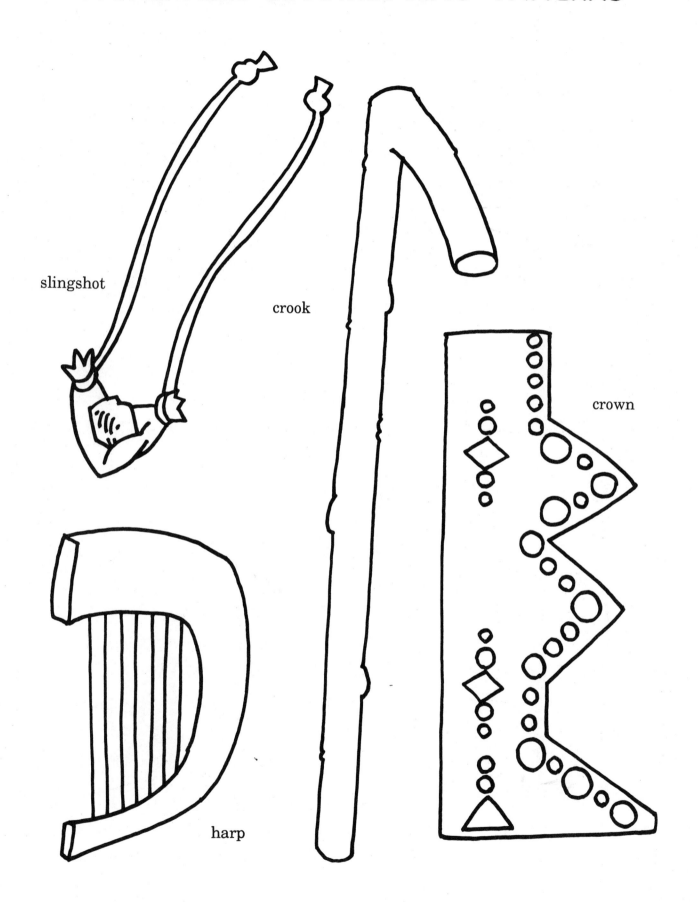

slingshot

crook

crown

harp

SS2875

"FAITHFUL DANIEL" PATTERNS

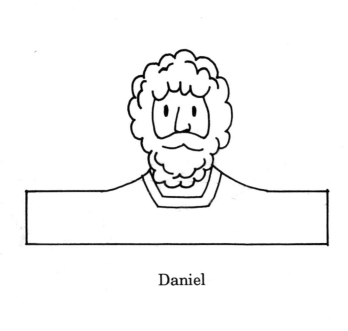

Daniel

Darius

angel

lion

SS2875

"A PROPHET WHO RAN AWAY" PATTERNS

ship

Jonah

fish

SS2875

"THE SNEAKY SNAKE" PATTERNS

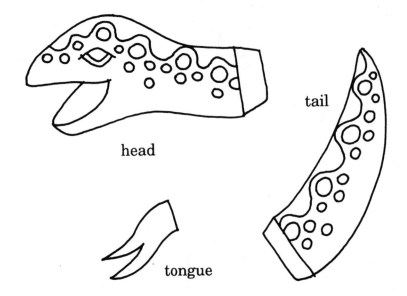

head

tail

tongue

God's Rules

You shall have no other gods before me.

You shall not make yourself an idol.

You shall not misuse the name of the Lord your God.

Remember the Sabbath day by keeping it holy.

Honor your father and your mother.

You shall not murder.

You shall not commit adultery.

You shall not steal.

You shall not give false testimony.

You shall not covet.

SS2875

"GIDEON, THE GENERAL" PATTERNS

trumpet

jar

"A DOVE FROM HEAVEN" PATTERN

dove

sheep

"THE LOST SHEEP" PATTERN

SS2875

"THE SEED PLANTER" PATTERNS

birds eating

sun wilting and
planted in rocks

weeds and
thorns

thriving
plant

SS2875

"THANK YOU, JESUS" PATTERN

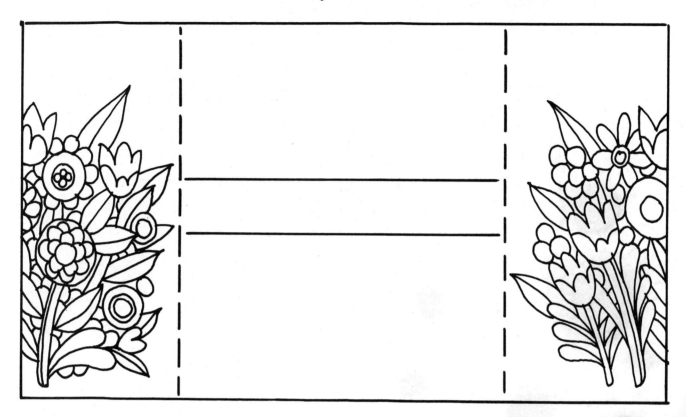

"TWO HOUSEBUILDERS" PATTERN

"JESUS LIVES!" PATTERNS

CUT

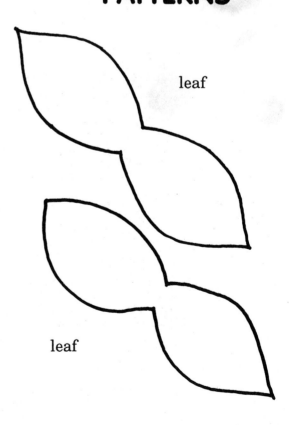

leaf

leaf

SS2875

"THE LAST SUPPER" PATTERNS

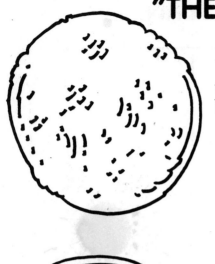

unleavened
bread

roasted
lamb

sauce

wine

bitter
herbs

"SO GREAT A LOVE" PATTERN

SS2875